Tarla Dalal India's # 1 Cookery Author

The
Rajasthani
Cookbook

S&C
SANJAY & CO.
MUMBAI

Other Books By Tarla Dalal

MINI SERIES

Idlis & Dosas	Curries & Kadhis
Cooking under 10 minutes	Chinese Recipes
Pizzas and Pasta	Jain Desi Khana
Fun Food for Children	7 Dinner Menus
Roz Ka Khana	Jain International Recipes
Microwave - Desi Khana	Punjabi Subzis
Paneer	Corn
Parathas	Microwave Subzis
Chawal	Baked Dishes
Dals	Stir-Fry
Chips & Dips	Potatoes New
Sandwiches	Recipes Using Leftovers New
Quick Cooking	Noodles New
	Lebenese New

TOTAL HEALTH

Low Calorie Healthy Cooking	Healthy Juices
Pregnancy Cookbook	Low Cholesterol Recipes
Baby and Toddler Cookbook	Good Food for Diabetes
Cooking with 1 Teaspoon of Oil	Healthy Subzis
Home Remedies	Healthy Snacks for Kids
Delicious Diabetic Recipes	High Blood Pressure Cook Book
Fast Foods Made Healthy	Low Calorie Sweets
Healthy Soups & Salads	Nutritious Recipes for Pregnancy
Healthy Breakfast	Diabetic Snacks
Calcium Rich Recipes	Zero Oil Rotis & Subzis New
Healthy Heart Cook Book	Zero Oil Soups, Salads & Snacks New
Forever Young Diet	Zero Oil Dal & Chawal New
Healthy Snacks	Acidity Cook Book New
Iron Rich Recipes	

INDIAN COOKING

Tava Cooking
Rotis & Subzis
Desi Khana
The Complete Gujarati Cook Book
Mithai
Chaat
Achaar aur Parathe
Swadisht Subzian
Punjabi Khana New

WESTERN COOKING

The Complete Italian Cookbook
The Chocolate Cookbook
Eggless Desserts
Mocktails & Snacks
Soups & Salads
Mexican Cooking
Chinese Cooking
Easy Chinese Cooking
Thai Cooking

GENERAL COOKING

Exciting Vegetarian Cooking
Microwave Recipes
Quick & Easy Cooking
Saatvik Khana
The Pleasures of Vegetarian Cooking
The Delights of Vegetarian Cooking
The Joys of Vegetarian Cooking
Cooking with Kids
Snacks Under 10 Minutes
Ice-Cream & Frozen Desserts
Desserts Under 10 Minutes
Entertaining
Microwave Snacks & Desserts

Fifth Printing : 2007

ISBN 10 : 81-86469-66-4
ISBN 13 : 978-8-186469-66-8

Price Rs. 230/-

Published & distributed by
SANJAY & COMPANY
A-1, 353 Shah & Nahar Industrial Estate, Dhanraj Mill Compound, Lower Parel (W), Mumbai 400 013, INDIA.
Tel: (91-22) 2496 8068 / Fax: (91-22) 2496 5876 / Email: sanjay@tarladalal.com / Website: www.tarladalal.com

UK and USA customers can call us on :
UK : 02080029533 • USA : 213-634-1406
For books, Membership on **tarladalal.com**, Subscription for **Cooking & More** and Recipe queries
Timing : 9.30 a.m. to 7.00 p.m. (IST), from Monday to Saturday
Local call charges applicable

Recipe Research & Production Design	**Illustrations**	**Design**	**Printed by**
Pinky Dixit	Ganesh Tayde	Satyamangal Rege	Minal Sales Agencies, Mumbai
Arati Fedane			
Jyoti Jain			

introduction

Rajasthan — the land of rajas and maharajas was where the royalty ensured the development of a variety of beautiful arts and crafts… and of an array of mouth-watering food traditions. The cuisine of this state resonates with vitality and good cheer, despite the fact that its people have to struggle hard to draw up even simple menus from one of the harshest terrains of India.

There is much more to Rajasthani cuisine than its signature dish, the ubiquitous Dal Baati Churma, page 102. Vegetarian Rajasthani food has a dazzling range of subtle and satisfying dishes like Gavarfali ki Subji, page 37, Ker Sangri, page 36, Panchmel ki Subji, page 44, and so on. The accent in their vegetarian cuisine is on purity of ingredients and on richness (ghee, mava and exotica). To their credit, this community has balanced this penchant for rich foods with the appropriate use of digestives, especially asafoetida, black salt, ginger and ajwain. They have an astounding variety of tongue tickling snacks like Pyaz ki Kachori, page 20, Stuffed Dahi Vadas, page 14, amongst others. And tea-time crispies like Bikaneri Bhujia, page 30, Masala Mathri, page 31, and Suhaali, page 13.

Rajasthani cooking in general has its own special flavour where the simplest and most basic ingredients go into the making of exotic recipes. The harsh climate, scarce rainfall and the non-availability of ingredients (especially greens) have a profound influence on the cuisine. Due to this scarcity, whatever vegetables are grown are often sun-dried so that they can be used for the rest of the year. In the Marwar region i.e. Bikaner, Jaisalmer and Barmer, cooking is done using minimal water and instead milk, buttermilk and ghee are used. Gram flour is extensively used to cook up delicacies such as Gatte ki Kadhi, page 60, Pithore Kadhi, page 62 and the famous Rajasthani Kadhi or 'khatta', page 65. Sun-dried mangodis and papad are used to whip up interesting recipes such as Papad Mangodi ki Subji, page 39. And bajra and corn are used all over the state to prepare dishes like Bajra Khichdi, page 86, Raabdi with Bajra Rotis, page 112, and Mooli Makai ki Roti, page 83.

Moreover, Rajasthani food has plenty of delectable mithais to satisfy your sweet cravings like the melt in the mouth Ghevar with Rabdi, page 122, Badam ka Halwa, page 125, Atte ka Malpua, page 121, Mava Kachori, page 133.

All the recipes in this book have been adapted to suit a variety of tastes and palates. Ghee and oil quantities have been limited while retaining the same traditional taste and mystique of the flavouful Rajasthani cuisine. Moreever, I wish to sincerely thank Mr. Tushar Bhandari, Heritage Resorts, Udaipur and Chef Vernon Coelho, Institute of Hotel Management, Mumbai for providing us invaluable inputs during the making of this book.

I am sure you will be able to whip up a scrumptious Rajasthani fare with these easy to follow recipes to surprise your family and friends.

Happy Cooking!

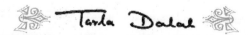

commonly used ingredients

 Ker and sangri (sanger)...

are wild berries (ker) and beans (sangri), that grow abundantly in the arid desert climate and are dried so that they can be stored for the year. Both ker and sangri are not exotic vegetables, but are wild berries (or beans) that grow independently and abundantly in the vast desert areas especially in Western Rajasthan—Jaisalmer and Barmer.

The story goes that ker and sangri were discovered ages ago by Rajasthani villagers during the time of a great famine when all other natural vegetation, which was scarce anyway, had died and withered away. But ker (small radish-like pods) and sangri (longish beans) flourished unconcernedly in the punishing Rajasthan sun. Intrigued by the appearance of these berries and delighted by their availability, the villagers took them home. There was no water for cooking because of the famine so the villagers dried the berries and cooked them in vegetable oil along with chillies and other spices.

Some household recipes also rehydrate the ker and sangri in buttermilk before cooking them, as it imparts a different flavour to the dish.

 Kachri and kachri powder...

is a fruit from the melon family which is bitter sweet in flavour. It grows abundantly in the desert region and is rarely cultivated as a crop. Kachri is dried and powdered for use and also to send to urban areas where it is not available.

Kachri powder has a sharp tangy taste and therefore it can sometimes be substituted with amchur powder but not for all recipes.

Kachri powder is also used as a tenderizer for barbecues and marinades.

 Mangodis...

are small dumplings made with seasoned moong dal paste. Shaped like small rounds or thin strands they are sun-dried and stored, to be preserved and used throughout the year. The intense desert sun helps to dry them rather quickly.

Mangodis are also made with other dals and pulses like moath, urad dal, etc. They are cooked with vegetables to make a vegetable dish or are cooked on their own to make a dal like dish that has a unique flavour.

 Bikaneri papads...

are a speciality of Bikaner in Rajasthan. These are a thicker variety of moong dal papads and are more fiery as they are seasoned with lots of crushed black pepper. Papads are used frequently in Rajasthani cooking to make a wide variety of dishes from subjis to a dry snack, like the Papad ki Churi, page 19, and are also relished with a meal. You will find these at some speciality stores, and in case you cannot find them, select any brand of pepper papad as a substitute.

In the past, all the womenfolk got together for the day to make these mangodis or papads and also catch up on their gossip. This tradition still exists in rural India and some enterprising women have also made a small industry of making both mangodis and papads.

 ## Khoya (mava)...

is prepared by boiling milk in a broad non-stick pan and reducing it to a semi-solid stage. There are two types of khoya depending upon the type of milk used and the moisture content in the finished product.

1. Sada Khoya (Mava) : Also called "Bhatti ka Khoya", it is made of full fat milk. It has a very low moisture content and is used to make barfis and laddus.

2. Hariyali Khoya (Hariyali Mava) : Also called "Chikna Khoya", it is made with low fat or cow's milk. It is slightly yellowish in colour and is loose and sticky in consistency. It has a higher moisture content than sada khoya and is used to make desserts like gulab jamun.

 ## Split mustard seeds (rai kuria)...

is also called yellow mustard dal. It is made from split and skinned mustard seeds. It is used for most savoury pickle recipes and imparts a hot and pungent flavour to the pickle besides providing tartness. Split mustard seeds are easily available at most provision stores.

 ## Split fenugreek seeds (methi kuria)...

are also called "methi na kuria" and are one of the popularly used pickling spices for savoury pickles. Crushed fenugreek seeds have a bitter after-taste and are therefore used in small quantities in most recipes. They can be made at home by coarsely grinding whole fenugreek (methi) seeds. They are available at most provision stores.

 ## Amchur slices and amchur...

are raw mango slices that are dried and preserved and are used to add sharpness to some dishes in place of tamarind or lemon juice. Slices are used in gravies, curries and chutneys and launjis.

Amchur slices that are powdered are easier to use in cooking as the flavour disperses evenly in the dish.

Amchur (dry mango powder) is a very important ingredient in the making of the ever-popular chaat masala.

index

Swadbhara Naashta

Swadisht Subji

Kadhi aur Dal

Roti, Puri aur Paratha

Khichdi aur Pulao

Achaar aur Launji

Traditional Combinations

Manpasand Mithai

Basic Recipe

Swadhara Naashta

amlana

Preparation time :
20 minutes.

No Cooking.

Serves 4.

A delicious appetiser that can be served along with a meal or at any time of the day as a cooling refresher in the hot desert summers.

Sweetened tamarind water spiked with black salt, pepper and cardamom powder. Serve this drink topped with plenty of ice cubes to thoroughly enjoy its sweet and tangy flavours.

2 tablespoons tamarind (imli)
8 to 10 tablespoons powdered sugar
¼ teaspoon pepper powder
¼ teaspoon cardamom (elaichi) powder
½ teaspoon black salt (sanchal)
salt to taste
3 cups chilled water
ice cubes to serve

For the garnish
1 tablespoon chopped mint leaves

1. Soak the tamarind in 1 cup of water for approx. 2 hours. Crush the tamarind and sieve the pulp through a muslin cloth. Squeeze out all the tamarind pulp.
2. Add the sugar, pepper powder, cardamom, black salt, salt and 3 cups of chilled water and mix well.
   Serve chilled, garnished with the chopped mint leaves and topped with ice cubes.

kairi ka pani

Preparation time :
5 minutes.

Cooking time :
15 to 20 minutes.

Serves 4 to 6.

An excellent summer cooler. It is also called 'panha' in most other regions of India.

A delicacy made of boiled raw mangoes has an added zing of black salt, cumin and ginger powder. Kairi ka pani can be had either sweetened or salted according to preference. This coolant drink is supposed to protect the human body from dehydration during the severe heat waves that hit the region during summer.

2 medium sized raw mangoes
¾ cup sugar
1 teaspoon roasted cumin seed (jeera) powder
1 teaspoon black salt (sanchal)
¼ teaspoon ginger powder (soonth)
salt to taste

1. Boil the raw mangoes in water till they are very soft.
2. Drain all the water and remove the skin from the mangoes.
3. Strain the mango pulp.
4. Add the sugar, cumin seed powder, black salt, ginger powder and salt and mix well.
5. Store in a bottle and refrigerate.
6. When you wish to serve, put 2 tablespoons of the mixture into a glass and top up with chilled water.

 handy tip If you wish to make the sweetened version add ½ teaspoon cardamom powder and a few saffron strands instead of the cumin powder and black salt.

thandai

Picture on page 25

Preparation time :
3 to 4 hours.

Cooking time :
10 minutes.

Makes 6 glasses.

Thandai is a very popular drink in Rajasthan. This famous dry fruit and saffron flavoured milk is traditionally prepared as an offering to Lord Shiva during the festival of Mahashivratri. Thandai is popular all over North India as well. It is often mixed with 'bhang' to make an intoxicating drink.

1 litre full fat milk
½ cup powdered sugar
10 to 12 peppercorns
a few saffron strands

To be ground into a fine powder
¼ cup almonds
2 tablespoons poppy seeds (khus khus)
2 tablespoons fennel seeds (saunf)
½ teaspoon cardamom (elaichi) powder
20 nos. white peppercorns

1. Boil the milk and allow it to cool completely. Keep aside.
2. Add the ground powder and mix well. Refrigerate the mixture for 3 to 4 hours.
3. Strain the mixture through a sieve, add the sugar, peppercorns and saffron and mix well.
   Serve chilled.

suhaali

Preparation time :
10 minutes.

Cooking time :
20 minutes.

Makes 15 suhaalis.

Suhaalis were traditionally made for weddings and special occasions like holi, diwali etc. Today however, they are available throughout the year at 'namkeen shops'.

These crisp tea-time delights are also called 'mathis' or 'mathris' in Rajasthan. These can also be relished with a cup of hot masala tea or a dollop of mango pickle for a quick snack.

It is important to remember to fry these in hot oil over a very slow flame so that they cook on the insides and are golden brown on the outside without getting burnt.

1 cup plain flour (maida)
1 teaspoon ajwain (carom seeds)
1 teaspoon cumin seeds (jeera)
2 tablespoons ghee, melted
salt to taste

Other ingredients
oil for deep frying

1. Combine all the ingredients with enough water to make a soft dough. Knead well.
2. Divide the dough into 15 equal portions.
3. Roll out each portion on a floured surface into a 25 mm. (1") diameter circle of 6 mm. (¼") thickness.
4. Prick each suhaali with a fork at regular intervals.
5. Deep fry the suhaalis in hot oil over a very slow flame till they are golden brown in colour.
6. Drain on absorbent paper. Cool completely and store in an air-tight container.

stuffed dahi vadas

Picture on page 103

Preparation time :
30 minutes.

Cooking time :
20 minutes.

Makes 10 dahi vadas.

Dahi vadas are eaten all over India. But Marwaris have glorified and enriched this simple lentil preparation by stuffing them with an assortment of dry fruits like cashews, sultanas etc. Jodhpuris and Marwaris often use moong dal instead of urad dal for the vadas.

Rajasthanis relish dahi vadas at any time of the day—as a snack or as an accompaniment to a main meal.

Making stuffed dahi vadas may seem complicated the first time you try them. But they can be very easily prepared as they are eaten and believe me, you will thoroughly enjoy them! Just follow the diagrams given at the end of the recipe on page 16.

You can prepare the vadas a day in advance and store them refrigerated. Soak the vadas in hot water and just before serving, drain them and squeeze out any excess water, before you add the curds.

For the vadas
¾ cup urad dal (split black lentils)
¼ teaspoon asafoetida (hing)
a pinch soda bi-carb
salt to taste

To be mixed together into a stuffing
2 tablespoons cashewnuts, chopped
2 tablespoons sultanas (kismis)
1 teaspoon ginger-green chilli paste

Other ingredients
oil for deep frying

For serving
1 cup fresh curds, beaten
a pinch black salt (sanchal)
2 tablespoons sugar
salt to taste

For the garnish
chilli powder
roasted cumin seed (jeera) powder
chopped coriander

1. Clean, wash and soak the urad dal for 2 to 3 hours.
2. Drain out all the water. Grind the urad dal to a coarse paste in a blender using a little water.
3. Add the asafoetida, salt, soda bi-carb and approx. 3 tablespoons of water to the urad dal paste and mix well with your hands.
4. Spread 2 tablespoons of the urad dal paste onto a 125 mm. x 125 mm. (5" x 5") piece of wet muslin cloth and form a 50 mm. (2") diameter circle (using wet hands).
5. Place ½ teaspoon of the stuffing in the centre of the urad dal paste and fold the muslin cloth over in the centre to make a semi-circle (as shown in the diagram on page 16).
6. Seal the edges of the semi-circle. Carefully open the muslin cloth and place the stuffed vada on your fingertips (wet your hands before).
7. Carefully slide the stuffed vada into a kadhai filled with hot oil and deep fry about 4 to 5 vadas at a time over a medium flame till they are golden brown.
8. Drain and soak the vadas in water for about 45 minutes.

How to proceed
1. Mix the curds, black salt, sugar and salt together. Keep aside.
2. Just before serving, squeeze out any excess water from the vadas by gently pressing each one between your palms. Arrange the vadas on a serving dish.
3. Pour the curds over the vadas. Sprinkle chilli powder, cumin seed powder and coriander on top.
   Serve immediately.

Diagram on next page

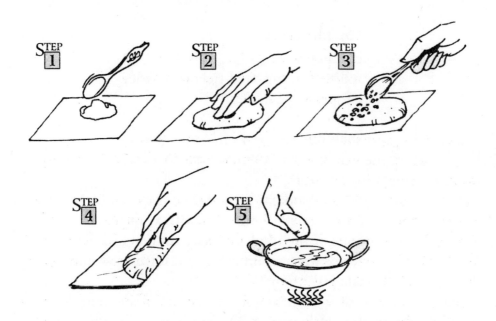

muttar ki kachori

Preparation time :
15 minutes.

Cooking time :
30 minutes.

Makes 12 kachoris.

Spicy green pea stuffed flaky and crisp kachoris.
Enjoy these kachoris topped with fresh curds and sweet chutney for a hearty evening snack.

Cook the stuffed kachoris lightly over a hot tava (griddle) on both sides and then deep fry them in hot oil over a slow flame. Kachoris made this way can be deep fried quickly in large batches and also use a lesser amount of oil while frying. You can prepare these kachoris ahead of time and warm them up in an oven just before serving.

For the dough (crust)
2 cups plain flour (maida)
¼ cup melted ghee
½ teaspoon salt

For the green pea filling
2 cups green peas
1 teaspoon green chillies, chopped
1 teaspoon ginger, grated
½ teaspoon nigella seeds (kalonji)
2 teaspoons fennel seeds (saunf)

16

2 bay leaves
1 teaspoon chilli powder
1 teaspoon garam masala
4 tablespoons chopped coriander
2 tablespoons oil
salt to taste

Other ingredients
oil for deep frying

For the dough (crust)
1. Combine all the ingredients and knead into a semi-soft dough using enough water. Knead well for 5 to 7 minutes.
2. Divide the dough into 12 equal parts and keep covered under a wet muslin cloth.

For the green pea filling
1. Coarsely grind the green peas, green chillies and ginger in a blender without using any water. Keep aside.
2. Heat the oil in a pan, add the nigella seeds, fennel seeds, bay leaves and ground green pea mixture and sauté over a very slow flame for 8 to 10 minutes.
3. Add the chilli powder, garam masala, coriander and salt and sauté for 2 more minutes. Remove the bay leaves and discard. Divide into 12 equal portions.

How to proceed
1. Roll out each portion of the dough into a 50 mm. (2") diameter circle.
2. Place one portion of the green pea filling in the centre of the rolled dough circle.
3. Surround the filling with the dough by slowly stretching it over the filling.
4. Seal the edges tightly and remove any excess dough.
5. Roll each filled portion into a 62 mm. (2½") diameter circle taking care to ensure that the filling does not spill out.
6. Gently press the centre of the kachori with your thumb.
7. Repeat for the remaining dough and green pea filling to make 11 more kachoris.

8. Deep fry in hot oil over low heat until golden brown on both sides. The kachori should puff up like puris. These take a long time to fry as the crust is thick and needs to be cooked on the insides also.
Serve hot. Alternatively, cool completely and store in an air-tight container. These will last for a day or two.

kalmi vadas

Preparation time :
10 minutes.

Cooking time :
15 minutes.

Serves 4.

Rajasthani food is as colourful and diverse as its glorious heritage. Rajasthanis are very fond of eating and this is reflected in the vast repetoire of recipes that they have devised out of fairly ordinary ingredients.
Kalmi vadas are deep fried gram dal crispies that can be enjoyed with a fiery green chutney.
You can prepare large vadas as in this recipe ahead of time and double fry (re-fry) them just before serving. These are perfect as a tea-time or pre-dinner snack.

½ cup split Bengal gram (chana dal)
1 teaspoon ginger-green chilli paste
¼ cup onions, finely chopped
½ teaspoon chilli powder
1 teaspoon coriander (dhania) seeds, roasted and crushed
1 teaspoon fennel seeds (saunf)
salt to taste

Other ingredients
oil for deep frying

1. Clean, wash and soak the chana dal overnight. Drain completely.
2. Without using any water, grind the soaked chana dal in a blender to make a smooth paste.
3. Add the ginger-green chilli paste, onions, chilli powder, coriander seeds, fennel seeds and salt and mix well.
4. Divide the mixture into 5 equal portions.
5. Take a big katori or a cup and tie a wet muslin cloth around it tightly (as shown in the diagram on the next page).

6. Sprinkle a little water over the muslin cloth and then place one portion of the chana dal mixture on it.
7. Flatten the chana dal mixture lightly using wet fingers to make a 100 mm. (4") diameter vada of 6 mm. (¼") thickness.
8. Heat oil in a kadhai, slide the vada in the hot oil and deep fry over a medium flame till light brown colour.
9. Repeat steps 6 to 8 to make 4 more vadas.
10. Cut the vadas into long strips and deep fry again till they are golden brown and crisp. Drain on absorbent paper.
    Serve hot with green chutney.

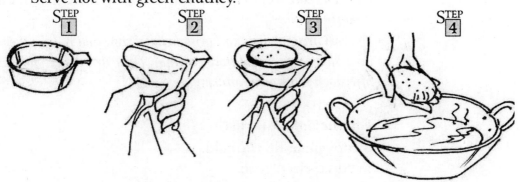

STEP 1   STEP 2   STEP 3   STEP 4

papad ki churi

Picture on page 26

Preparation time :
5 minutes.

Cooking time :
5 minutes.

Serves 3 to 4.

Another favourite Marwari snack that often accompanies meals. As the name suggests, it is a preparation of crushed papads which are tossed in spices and ghee. I have added some Bikaneri bhujia to this recipe to provide extra crunch. Bikaneri papads are a thicker and fierier variety of papads and are better for use in this recipe as they do not get soggy very fast. You will find these at some speciality stores.

4 large Bikaneri papads, roasted and crushed
½ cup onions, finely chopped
2 tablespoons chopped coriander
2 teaspoons chilli powder
1 tablespoon melted ghee
¼ cup Bikaneri bhujia, page 30
salt to taste

Combine all the ingredients in a bowl and toss well. Serve immediately.

pyaz ki kachori

Picture on page 25

Preparation time :
15 minutes.

Cooking time :
30 minutes.

Makes 12 kachoris.

These kachoris probably originated in Jodhpur but are today popular throughout Rajasthan.

Very few households actually prepare these crisp, flaky deep fried kachoris stuffed with a lightly caramalised and exceptionally seasoned onion filling. Steaming hot pyaz ki kachoris or aloo pyaz ki kachoris are sold at most 'namkeen' shops in Rajasthan.

Like all kachoris, they are eaten with a sweet and spicy tamarind chutney.

You can prepare these kachoris ahead of time and re-heat them in a slow oven just before serving. They are perfect for an afternoon snack on a rainy day.

For the dough (crust)
2 cups plain flour (maida)
¼ cup melted ghee
½ teaspoon salt

For the onion filling
2 cups onions, finely chopped
1 teaspoon nigella seeds (kalonji)
2 teaspoons fennel seeds (saunf)
2 bay leaves
1½ teaspoons green chillies, finely chopped
2 tablespoons Bengal gram flour (besan)
2 teaspoons coriander (dhania) powder
2 teaspoons chilli powder
1 teaspoon garam masala
3 tablespoons chopped coriander
2 tablespoons oil
salt to taste

Other ingredients
oil for deep frying

For the dough (crust)

1. Combine all the ingredients in a bowl and knead into semi-soft dough using enough water. Knead well for 5 to 7 minutes.
2. Divide the dough into 12 equal parts and keep covered under a wet muslin cloth.

For the onion filling

1. Heat the oil in a pan. Add the nigella seeds, fennel seeds, bay leaves, green chillies and onions and sauté till the onions turn light brown in colour.
2. Add the gram flour, coriander powder, chilli powder, garam masala and salt and sauté for 2 to 3 minutes.
3. Add the chopped coriander and mix well. Remove the bay leaves and discard. Allow the mixture to cool completely.
4. Divide into 12 equal portions and keep aside.

How to proceed

1. Roll out each portion of the dough into a 50 mm. (2") diameter circle.
2. Place one portion of the onion filling in the centre of the rolled dough circle.
3. Surround the filling with the dough by slowly stretching it over the filling.
4. Seal the ends tightly and remove any excess dough.
5. Roll each filled portion into a 62 mm. (2½") diameter circle taking care to ensure that the filling does not spill out.
6. Gently press the centre of the kachori with your thumb.
7. Repeat with the remaining dough and filling to make 11 more kachoris.
8. Deep fry the kachoris in hot oil over a slow flame till golden brown.The kachoris should puff up like puris. These take a long time to fry as the crust is thick and needs to be cooked in the insides also. Serve hot with chutney.

stuffed chilas

Preparation time :
20 minutes.

Cooking time :
20 minutes.

Makes 12 chilas.

Chilas are pancakes that are unique to the desert province of Rajasthan.

This recipe is of gram flour chilas stuffed with cubes of paneer, green peas and tangy tomatoes, tossed together with a dash of chilli and cumin seeds.

At home, we often make besan chilas with onions, tomatoes, coriander and chillies. This recipe however transforms the same old chila into a delightful chaat for your family and friends.

For the chilas

1 cup Bengal gram flour (besan)
a pinch asafoetida (hing)
1 tablespoon oil
salt to taste
oil for cooking

For the stuffing

2 cups paneer (cottage cheese), cubed
1 cup green peas, boiled
½ cup tomatoes, chopped
1 green chilli, chopped
½ teaspoon cumin seeds (jeera)
1 teaspoon chaat masala
2 tablespoons chopped coriander
1 tablespoon butter
salt to taste

For the chilas

1. Mix the gram flour, asafoetida, salt and 1 tablespoon of oil to make a thin batter, using enough water.
2. Heat a non-stick tava (griddle) and lightly grease it with oil.
3. Pour a ladleful of the mixture on the tava and spread it evenly to make a thin pancake.

4. Cook on both sides over a medium flame using a little oil, taking care to see that the chila does not brown.
5. Repeat for the remaining batter to make 12 chilas. Keep aside.

For the stuffing mixture
1. Heat the butter and add the green chilli and cumin seeds.
2. Add the tomatoes and sauté for 2 to 3 minutes.
3. Add the paneer, peas, chaat masala and salt and sauté for a few more minutes.
4. Top with the chopped coriander, divide into 12 portions and keep aside.

How to proceed
1. Place one portion of the stuffing mixture on a chila and fold it to make a semi-circle.
2. Repeat with the remaining chilas and stuffing.
3. Top with green chutney and serve hot.

kanji vadas

Preparation time :
1 day.

Cooking time :
15 minutes.

Serves 4.

This is a Marwari delicacy of moong dal vadas immersed in a tangy mustard flavoured liquid. The 'kanji' or 'Rai ka Pani' as it is known needs to be prepared a day in advance so that all the flavours mellow down. The vadas are added the following day.

Kanji vadas are a popular snack sold on the streets throughout Rajasthan.

Chukandar (beetroot) kanji is also popular and is specially prepared for the festival of Holi. Instead of moong dal vadas, large chunks of beetroot are marinated in 'Rai ka Pani' or 'Rai ka Achaar' to give it a rich red colour.

Serve plenty of kanji with the vadas so that you can enjoy a large sip of the kanji once the vadas are polished off.

For the kanji

¼ cup split mustard seeds (rai na kuria)
1 tablespoon black salt (sanchal)
1½ teaspoons chilli powder
salt to taste

For the vadas

2½ cups soaked yellow moong dal (split yellow gram)
1 teaspoon ginger-green chilli paste
½ teaspoon fennel seeds (saunf)
¼ teaspoon asafoetida (hing)
salt to taste

1) **Bikaneri Bhujia,** *page 30*
2) **Masala Mathri,** *page 31*
3) **Pyaz ki Kachori,** *page 20*
4) **Thandai,** *page 12*

Other ingredients
oil for deep frying

For the kanji
1. Combine all the ingredients and grind to a fine powder.
2. Dissolve this powder in 1½ litres of water, cover and keep refrigerated for 24 hours to allow all the flavours to blend.

For the vadas
1. Drain and grind the moong dal to a coarse paste without using water.
2. Add the ginger-green chilli paste, fennel seeds, asafoetida and salt and mix well.
3. Wet your hands, take 2 tablespoons of the dal paste on your palm or on a sheet of wet plastic and shape into a 25 mm. (1") diameter circle.
4. Repeat with the remaining paste.
5. Deep fry the circles in hot oil over a medium flame till golden brown in colour.
6. Drain on absorbent paper and cool.

How to proceed
1. Soak the vadas in water for approx. 1 hour. Drain and squeeze out all the water by pressing each vada gently between your palms.
2. Place the vadas in the kanji and allow them to soak for at least 1 hour. Serve chilled.

 note During the cold weather, you need not refrigerate the kanji once it is made.

1) **Gatte ki Kadhi,** *page 60*
2) **Khoba Roti,** *page 84*
3) **Ker Sangri,** *page 36*
4) **Papad ki Churi,** *page 19*

27

khasta kachori

Preparation time :
15 minutes.

Cooking time :
30 minutes.

Makes 12 kachoris.

A perfect kachori is one that is puffed up and flaky outside but hollow inside as the filling sticks to the crust.

'Khasta' actually means 'flaky' and this flaky kachori is filled with a delectable moong dal mixture and deep fried. Remember to fry the kachori on a very slow flame so that the crust is crisp and gets cooked on the inside.

This dish can be stored in air-tight containers for upto a week. When unexpected guests arrive, warm up the kachoris in a slow oven for about 7 to 10 minutes fill them with curds and chutneys and serve.

For the dough (crust)
2 cups plain flour (maida)
¼ cup melted ghee
½ teaspoon salt

For the filling
½ cup yellow moong dal (split yellow gram), soaked for 4 hours
1 teaspoon cumin seeds (jeera)
¼ teaspoon asafoetida (hing)
1 teaspoon ginger-green chilli paste
1 teaspoon chilli powder
1 teaspoon garam masala
1 tablespoon amchur (dry mango powder)
2 tablespoons Bengal gram flour (besan)
3 tablespoons oil
salt to taste

Other ingredients
oil for deep frying

For the dough (crust)

1. Combine all the ingredients and knead into a semi-soft dough using enough water. Knead very well for 5 to 7 minutes.
2. Divide the dough into 12 equal parts and keep covered under a wet muslin cloth.

For the filling

1. Drain the soaked moong dal. Heat the oil in a pan and add the cumin seeds and asafoetida.
2. When the seeds crackle, add the drained moong dal and sauté for a few seconds.
3. Add the ginger-green chilli paste, chilli powder, garam masala, amchur, gram flour and salt and stir for 5 to 7 minutes till the masalas are cooked.
4. Cool and divide into 12 equal portions. Shape each portion into an even sized round and keep aside.

How to proceed

1. Roll out each portion of the dough into a 50 mm. (2") diameter circle.
2. Place one portion of the filling mixture in the centre of the rolled dough circle.
3. Surround the filling mixture with the dough by slowly stretching it over the filling mixture.
4. Seal the ends tightly and remove any excess dough.
5. Roll each filled portion into a 62 mm. (2½") diameter circle taking care to ensure that the filling does not spill out.
6. Gently press the centre of the kachori with your thumb.
7. Repeat with the remaining dough and filling to make 11 more kachoris.
8. Deep fry the kachoris in hot oil over a slow flame till golden brown on both sides. The kachoris should puff up like puris. These take a long time to fry as the crust is thick and needs to be cooked on the inside also.
9. Cool and keep aside or store in an air-tight container.

bikaneri bhujia

Picture on page 25

Preparation time :
10 minutes.

Cooking time :
15 minutes.

Serves 6 to 8.

Bikaner is known for this savoury snack. Deep fried bhujia (i.e. vermicelli or sev) is usually made of gram flour but a variety of flours like moong, moath and even mashed potatoes are used to make different kinds of bhujia.

A large number of shops all over the country sell Bikaneri bhujia which are as celebrated as the Rasgullas of Bengal.

Bikaneri bhujia is spicy — usually black pepper is used to add fire to this preparation.

A large quantity of bhujia can be made and stored for several days in air-tight containers.

½ cup moath (matki) flour
½ cup Bengal gram flour (besan)
1½ teaspoons pepper powder
¼ teaspoon cardamom (elaichi) powder
¼ teaspoon asafoetida (hing)
1 teaspoon oil
salt to taste

Other ingredients
oil for deep frying

1. Combine all the ingredients and mix well to form a soft dough using enough water.
2. Heat the oil in a kadhai, put the dough in a "sev" press and squeeze by hand through the "sev" press into the hot oil.
3. Deep fry the bhujia over a medium flame till is lightly browned. Drain on absorbent paper.
4. Repeat steps 2 and 3 till all the dough is used up. Cool and store the bhujia in an air-tight container.

masala mathri

Picture on page 25

Preparation time :
30 minutes.

Cooking time :
45 minutes.

Makes 5 mathris.

Rajasthani cooking has been influenced by the war-like lifestyle of its inhabitants and the ingredients available in this region. Food that will last for several days and that can be eaten without heating was preferred, more out of necessity than choice. Crispy, flaky and superbly flavoured deep fried 'mathris' or 'mathis' have probably emerged from this style of cooking. This popular 'any time' snack can be stored for several days.

Mathris are eaten with a spicy mango or lemon pickle and are often served with tea. Sometimes they even form part of an easy breakfast with milk.

Large mathris — plain or stuffed — are pinched on their surface with floral and other intricate designs and they are a 'must' for all occasions including marriages, poojas etc.

Rajasthanis are fond of storing large jars of mathris which they can munch at any time of the day.

For the dough
1 cup plain flour (maida)
2 tablespoons melted ghee
salt to taste

For the filling
¼ cup Bengal gram flour (besan)
½ teaspoon cumin seeds (jeera)
¼ teaspoon ajwain (carom seeds)
1 teaspoon chilli powder
3 teaspoons oil
salt to taste

Other ingredients
oil or ghee for deep frying

For the dough

1. Combine the plain flour, ghee, salt and enough water to make a semi-soft dough. Knead well.
2. Cover the dough with a wet muslin cloth and keep aside.

For the filling

1. Combine all the ingredients and sauté over a slow flame till the gram flour turns golden brown in colour.
2. Cool completely and divide the filling into 5 equal portions. Keep aside.

How to proceed

1. Divide the dough into 5 equal portions.
2. Roll out each portion of the dough into a 50 mm. (2") diameter circle.
3. Place one portion of the filling in the centre of each rolled dough circle and bring the ends together so as to seal the filling inside completely.
4. Roll out the stuffed dough circle to make a 100 mm. (4") diameter circle taking care to ensure the filling does not spill out.
5. Pinch the sides of the mathri using your fingertips (as shown in the diagram on the next page).
6. Pinch the surface of the rolled out mathri so as to form a design.
7. Prick the mathri all over with a fork (please refer to the diagram).
8. Repeat steps 2 to 7 with the remaining portions of the dough and filling.
9. Deep fry the mathris in hot oil till they are half cooked. Drain.
10. Once all the mathris are half-cooked, deep fry them over a slow flame till they are golden brown in colour. These take a long time to fry as the crust is thick and needs to be cooked on the insides also.
11. Drain on absorbent paper.
12. Cool and store in an air-tight container.
    Serve with pickle or masala tea.

VARIATION : *plain mathri*

You can make the masala mathris without the filling to make plain mathris.

Refer to picture on page 25

shakkar para

Preparation time :
15 minutes.

Cooking time :
30 minutes.

Makes 60 pieces.

Deep fried wheat flour and sugar crispies. In Rajasthan, they are also called 'meethi mathri'. There are several tradtional ways of making these, but I find this recipe the easiest to follow.

Remember to fry them over a slow flame, as the insides need to be cooked too! I have cut the shakkar paras into small squares but you can also shape them like mathris, if you like.

1½ cups whole wheat flour (gehun ka atta)
¼ cup sugar
¼ cup milk
2 tablespoons ghee
a pinch salt

Other ingredients
ghee or oil for deep frying

1. Sieve the flour and salt together.
2. In a pan, combine the sugar, milk and ghee and bring to a boil. Allow the sugar to dissolve and cool completely.
3. Add this to the flour mixture, a little at a time. Knead into a firm dough.
4. Divide it into 2 equal portions and roll out each portion into 2 squares that are 6 mm. (¼") thick.
5. Prick the surface with a fork at regular intervals.
6. Cut into 25 mm. (1") diamond shaped pieces and allow to dry out for at least 30 minutes.
7. Deep fry in hot oil over a medium flame (so that they cook on the inside also).
8. Drain on absorbent paper. Cool completely and store in an air-tight container.

Swadisht Subji

ker sangri

Picture on page 26

Preparation time :
10 minutes.

Cooking time :
20 minutes.

Serves 4.

One of the great dishes of Rajasthani cuisine. This simple piquant and tangy vegetable preparation does not really reflect the richness of its colorful school of cooking. Because ker and sangri are not exotic vegetables, but are wild berries (or beans) that grow independently and abundantly in the vast desert areas especially in Western Rajasthan—Jaisalmer and Barmer.

The story goes that ker and sangri were discovered ages ago by Rajasthani villagers during the time of a great famine when all other natural vegetation, which was scarce anyways, had died and withered away. But ker (small, radish-like pods) and sangri (longish beans) flourished unconcernedly in the punishing sun. Intrigued by the appearance of these berries and delighted by their availability, the villagers took them home. There was no water for cooking because of the famine so the villagers dried the berries and cooked them in vegetable oil along with chillies and other spices. Voila! They had something wonderful to eat with their bajra (millet) rotis. Today, of course we cook them in water or butter milk. Incredibly, ker sangri continues to be prepared in this simple manner and is one of the mainstays of the Marwari kitchen and a 'must have' recipe on wedding menus even today.

Ker and sangri are available in the dried form and can be stored for a year at least. The smaller berries of ker are supposed to full of flavour and are therefore more expensive.

1 tablespoon ker
1 cup sangri (sanger)
½ teaspoon turmeric powder (haldi)
3 teaspoons chilli powder
2 teaspoons coriander (dhania) powder
1½ teaspoons amchur (dry mango powder)
1 teaspoon sultanas (kismis)
salt to taste

For the tempering
2 Kashmiri chillies

¼ teaspoon ajwain (carom seeds)
¼ teaspoon asafoetida (hing)
3 tablespoons oil

1. Combine the ker, sangri and salt with 2½ cups of water. Pressure cook for 3 whistles.
2. Drain out the water and add the turmeric powder, chilli powder, coriander powder, amchur, sultanas and salt, if required and mix well.
3. For the tempering, heat the oil in a pan and add the Kashmiri chillies, ajwain and asafoetida. When the seeds crackle, pour the tempering over the ker sangri mixture. Mix well and cook for a few minutes. Serve hot.

handy tip This spicy subji tastes good with puris, parathas or misi rotis.

gavarfali ki subji *Picture on page 52*

Preparation time : 15 minutes.

Cooking time : 15 minutes.

Serves 4.

Gavarfali or 'cluster beans' as they are also called, are an integeral part of Rajasthani cooking. They are always strung and boiled before use.

There are quite a few ways in which this vegetable is cooked. One way is with potatoes and dried spices. Another way is with a variety of other vegetables like Panchmel ki Subji on page 44. My favourite way is however, the one given below.

2 cups gavarfali (cluster beans)
1 cup fresh curds, beaten
1 tablespoon coriander (dhania) powder
2 teaspoons chilli powder
2 teaspoons Bengal gram flour (besan)
1 teaspoon cumin seeds (jeera)
½ teaspoon mustard seeds (rai)
¼ teaspoon asafoetida (hing)
1 teaspoon fennel seeds (saunf)
5 curry leaves
2 tablespoons oil
salt to taste

1. Clean the gavarfali by removing the ends and edged fibre (stringing them).
2. Pressure cook the gavarfali in water for 2 whistles and drain out all the water.
3. Combine the curds, coriander powder, chilli powder, gram flour and salt and whisk well.
4. Heat the oil in a pan and add the cumin seeds, mustard seeds, asafoetida and fennel seeds.
5. When the seeds crackle, add the curd mixture, curry leaves and ¼ cup of water and mix well.
6. Bring to a boil and simmer for 4 to 5 minutes, while stirring continously.
7. Add the gavarfali and mix well. Simmer for another 2 to 3 minutes. Serve hot with rotis.

aloo ki subji

Picture on cover

Preparation time :
10 minutes.

Cooking time :
10 minutes.

Serves 4.

The ever popular potato finds its way into every cuisine and is cooked in a different, delicious way each time.

This recipe cooks it in a tangy yoghurt gravy that is flavoured with fennel and nigella and other subtle spices.

Aloo ki Subji served with puris is a favourite breakfast combination washed down with hot masala tea.

4 cups potatoes, boiled, peeled and cubed
1 cup fresh curds, beaten
1 teaspoon Bengal gram flour (besan)
½ teaspoon mustard seeds (rai)
1 teaspoon cumin seeds (jeera)
1 teaspoon fennel seeds (saunf)
½ teaspoon nigella seeds (kalonji)
1 bay leaf
2 cloves
2 sticks cinnamon
⅛ teaspoon asafoetida (hing)
2 teaspoons chilli powder
¼ teaspoon turmeric powder (haldi)
1 teaspoon coriander-cumin seed (dhania-jeera) powder

1 tablespoon ghee
salt to taste

For the garnish
2 tablespoons chopped coriander

1. In a bowl, combine the curds and gram flour and whisk well. Keep aside.
2. Heat the ghee in a pan and add the mustard seeds. When they crackle, add the cumin seeds, fennel seeds, nigella seeds, bay leaf, cloves, cinnamon and asafoetida and stir for a few seconds.
3. Add the curds and gram flour mixture, chilli powder, turmeric powder, coriander-cumin seed powder and continue stirring till it comes to a boil.
4. Add the potatoes and salt with ½ cup of water and mix well. Bring to a boil.
   Serve hot, garnished with the coriander.

papad mangodi ki subji

Preparation time :
5 minutes.

Cooking time :
25 minutes.

Serves 4.

Mangodis are made with seasoned moong dal paste. Shaped like small rounds or thin strands they are sun-dried and stored for use throughout the year. The intense desert sun helps to dry them rather quickly. Nowdays, they are also available at most provision stores. In the past, all the womenfolk got together for the day to make these mangodis or papads and also catch up on their gossip. This tradition still exists in rural India and some enterprising women have also made a small industry of making both mangodis and papads. This recipe uses both these ingredients to make a tongue tickling dish that can be made in a jiffy and enjoyed with steamed rice or parathas.

1 cup moong dal mangodi, page 136
4 large urad dal papads (raw), torn into small pieces
1 cup fresh curds, beaten
2 teaspoons chilli powder
4 teaspoons coriander (dhania) powder

1 teaspoon amchur (dry mango powder)
¼ teaspoon turmeric powder (haldi)
1 teaspoon cumin seeds (jeera)
½ teaspoon mustard seeds (rai)
a pinch asafoetida (hing)
2 teaspoons ginger-green chilli paste
4 tablespoons oil
salt to taste

1. Crush the mangodis coarsely using a mortar and pestle.
2. Heat 2 tablespoons of oil in a pressure cooker, add the crushed mangodis and sauté for 2 to 3 minutes. Add 1 cup of water and pressure cook for 3 to 4 whistles until the mangodis are soft. Keep aside.
3. In a bowl, combine the curds, chilli powder, coriander powder, amchur and turmeric powder and whisk well.
4. Heat the remaining oil in a pan and add the cumin seeds and mustard seeds. When the seeds crackle, add the asafoetida, ginger-green chilli paste and sauté for a few seconds.
5. Add the curd mixture and salt and cook over a slow flame, while stirring continuously. Bring to a boil.
6. Add the mangodis (along with the water in which they were cooked) and papads and simmer for about 4 to 5 minutes.
Serve hot.

bharwa lauki

Picture on page 78

Preparation time :
20 minutes.

Cooking time :
30 minutes.

Serves 4.

Housewives in Rajasthan create exciting dishes out of what seem the most common vegetables, herbs and spices. This recipe is another such classic example.

Bottlegourd (or white pumpkin) stuffed with spicy paneer is tossed in a flavourful tomato based gravy. Although curds are used to prepare most Rajasthani gravies, the use of tomato provides an interesting twist and a delightful variation to recipes.

You can use boiled potatoes instead of paneer for the stuffing to make an altogether different recipe.

For the lauki

250 grams white pumpkin (doodhi or lauki)
½ teaspoon salt
2 tablespoons oil

To be mixed into a filling

½ cup paneer (cottage cheese), grated
¼ cup onions, finely chopped
1 teaspoon ginger-green chilli paste
2 tablespoons chopped coriander
½ teaspoon amchur (dry mango powder)
½ teaspoon coriander (dhania) powder
½ teaspoon chilli powder
¼ cup mixed dry fruits (cashewnuts, sultanas, almonds), finely chopped
1 teaspoon cornflour
salt to taste

For the gravy

3 medium tomatoes, puréed
1 small stick cinnamon
3 cloves
1 teaspoon ginger-green chilli paste
1 teaspoon coriander (dhania) powder

41

2 teaspoons chilli powder
½ teaspoon garam masala
1 teaspoon sugar
1 tablespoon oil
salt to taste

For the garnish
2 tablespoons chopped coriander

For the lauki
1. Peel the pumpkin and place it in a pressure cooker with 1 cup of water and the salt. Pressure cook for 1 whistle and cool.
2. Scoop out the inside pulp of the pumpkin. Discard the pulp and keep the scooped pumpkin aside.
3. Stuff the scooped out pumpkin shell with the filling mixture and keep aside.
4. Heat the oil in a pan and shallow fry the stuffed pumpkin till brown spots appear on all the sides. Remove and keep aside.

For the gravy
1. Heat the oil in a pan, add the cinnamon and cloves and fry for 1 minute. Add the tomato purée, ginger-green chilli paste, coriander powder, chilli powder, garam masala, sugar and salt and simmer till the oil separates.
2. Add ¼ cup of water and bring to a boil. Keep aside.

How to proceed
1. To serve, cut the stuffed pumpkin into 25 mm. (1") thick slices and place them on a serving dish.
2. Pour the hot gravy over stuffed the pumpkin slices.
3. Garnish with the coriander and serve hot.

dahi chane ki subji

Preparation time :
15 minutes.

Cooking time :
15 minutes.

Serves 4.

Also called 'Chane Jaisalmer Ke', this dish of red chana simmered in a curd gravy makes a wonderful accompaniment for either rice or bajra rotis.

Traditionally this is served with misi roti and makes a complete meal by providing calcium, proteins and carbohydrates to supplement a healthy diet.

When you add the curds and besan mixture into the chana, stir it continuously till it comes to a boil, so as to prevent the curd gravy from splitting.

1 cup red chana (whole red gram), soaked overnight and drained
½ teaspoon cumin seeds (jeera)
¼ teaspoon mustard seeds (rai)
2 bay leaves
4 whole red chillies
⅛ teaspoon asafoetida (hing)
1 teaspoon ginger-green chilli paste
1 teaspoon chilli powder
¼ teaspoon turmeric powder (haldi)
1 cup curds, beaten
2 teaspoons Bengal gram flour (besan)
4 tablespoons chopped coriander
1 tablespoon oil
salt to taste

1. Heat the oil in a pressure cooker and add the cumin seeds, mustard seeds, bay leaves, red chillies and asafoetida.
2. When the seeds crackle, add the red chana, ginger-green chilli paste, chilli powder, turmeric powder, salt and 2 cups of water. Pressure cook for 2 to 3 whistles till the chana is cooked.
3. Whisk the curds and gram flour together. Add the curd mixture to the cooked chana and bring to a boil while stirring continuously. Simmer for 4 to 5 minutes.

Serve hot, garnished with the coriander.

panchmel ki subji

Preparation time :
20 minutes.

Cooking time :
15 minutes.

Serves 4.

Panchmel is a district in Gujarat bordering Rajasthan. But the word 'panchmel' has been commonly used to denote a combination of five ingredients.

A judicious mix of five vegetables—gavarfali, chawli, capsicum, cucumber and carrots — constitute the panchmel of this mouth-watering recipe. Tossed in aromatic spices, this dry vegetable preparation tastes fantastic when served with rotis or bhakris.

Another distinct feature of this recipe and that of Rajasthani cooking is the use of amchur (dry mango powder) which enhances the tangy flavours of a dish in the absence of curds and tomatoes.

¾ cup gavarfali (cluster beans), chopped
¾ cup chawli (long beans), chopped
1 capsicum, chopped
1 cucumber, peeled and diced
2 carrots, peeled and diced
1 teaspoon cumin seeds (jeera)
2 teaspoons ginger-green chilli paste
1 teaspoon chilli powder
¼ teaspoon turmeric powder (haldi)
2 teaspoons coriander (dhania) powder
1 teaspoon amchur (dry mango powder)
2 tablespoons oil
salt to taste

1. Heat the oil in a non-stick pan, add the cumin seeds and ginger-green chilli paste and sauté for few seconds.
2. Add the gavarfali, chawli, capsicum, cucumber, carrots, chilli powder, turmeric powder, salt and ¼ cup of water. Cover and cook over a slow flame till the vegetables are cooked, stirring occassionally.
3. Add the coriander powder and amchur and mix well.
Serve hot.

methi mangodi

Picture on page 51

Preparation time :
10 minutes.

Cooking time :
25 minutes.

Serves 4.

Mangodis are sun-dried grape sized dumplings made from soaked and ground moong dal or sometimes from urad dal. Due to scarcity of vegetables, the ingenious Rajasthanis use different forms of pulses to whip up healthy and tasty meals. Mangodis or moong dal badis are often used to rustle up several tasty and mouth-watering recipes.
Fenugreek tossed mangodis is one such delightful recipe.
Serve this subji with hot phulkas and a spicy mango pickle.

1 bunch methi leaves (fenugreek leaves), chopped
½ cup moong dal mangodi, crushed, page 136
1 teaspoon turmeric powder (haldi)
½ teaspoon cumin seeds (jeera)
2 teaspoons ginger-green chilli paste
1 teaspoon coriander (dhania) powder
½ cup milk
½ cup curds, beaten
1 teaspoon sugar
4 tablespoons oil
salt to taste

1. Add salt and ½ teaspoon turmeric powder to the methi leaves and keep aside for 5 minutes. Squeeze out all the water and wash the methi leaves very well. Keep aside.
2. Heat the oil in a pressure cooker and add the cumin seeds.
3. When the seeds crackle, add the ginger-green chilli paste and stir for a few seconds.
4. Add the mangodi and sauté for 2 to 3 minutes.
5. Add the methi and sauté for 5 to 7 minutes over a slow flame.
6. Add the coriander powder, milk, curds, sugar, ½ teaspoon of turmeric powder, salt and ½ cup of water and bring to a boil while stirring continuously.
7. Pressure cook for 1 to 2 whistles or until the mangodis are soft and cooked.
   Serve hot.

gavarfali ki sukhi subji

Preparation time :
15 minutes.

Cooking time :
20 minutes.

Serves 4.

Due to scant rainfall, very few vegetables grow in Rajasthan. Gavarfali is one of the few commonly available and abundantly used vegetable in this region. There are several interesting ways in which gavarfali is cooked, mostly with potatoes to make a dry vegetable or in a curd based gravy.

This recipe uses dry masalas along with onions and garlic to spice up the gavarfali.

You can also add potatoes if you wish. Remember always to string the thicker gavarfali to get rid of its fibrous sides before using it for a dish.

2 cups gavarfali (cluster beans), cut into 25 mm. (1") pieces
a pinch soda bi-carb
½ teaspoon cumin seeds (jeera)
2 teaspoons ginger-green chilli paste
4 cloves garlic, crushed
½ cup onions, chopped
¼ teaspoon turmeric powder (haldi)
½ teaspoon coriander (dhania) powder
¼ teaspoon mustard powder
½ teaspoon chilli powder
3 tablespoons oil
salt to taste

1. Boil the gavarfali with soda bi-carb in water for about 5 to 7 minutes.
2. Drain, squeeze out all the water and keep aside.
3. Heat the oil in a pan and add the cumin seeds.
4. When the seeds crackle, add the ginger-green chilli paste and garlic and sauté for a few seconds.
5. Add the onions and sauté till they turn translucent.
6. Add the boiled gavarfali, turmeric powder, coriander powder, mustard powder, chilli powder and salt and sauté for 3 to 4 minutes.
Serve hot.

handy tip

Add ½ teaspoon kachri powder to the subji for better taste.
Trim the ends and string the gavarfali before cutting them into
small pieces for the above recipe.

arbi ka saag

Preparation time :
10 minutes.

Cooking time :
15 minutes.

Serves 4.

*This little known and scarcely used vegetable is converted into a
spicy dish —Rajasthani style with the addition of a blend of
spices.*

*The arbi can be boiled and sautéed too without deep frying
them, but I prefer the crispy texture of deep fried arbi.*

*A word of caution about handling arbi. Grease your hands
generously with oil before you start to peel or cut them as they
release a sticky fluid which is difficult to wash off. The oil forms a
layer on your palms, not allowing this fluid to come in contact
with your skin.*

1½ cups arbi (colocassia root), boiled, peeled and sliced
¼ teaspoon ajwain (carom seeds)
¼ teaspoon mustard seeds (rai)
¼ teaspoon turmeric powder (haldi)
½ teaspoon chilli powder
½ teaspoon coriander (dhania) powder
½ teaspoon lemon juice
1 teaspoon oil
salt to taste

Other ingredients
oil for deep frying

1. Heat the oil in a kadhai and deep fry the arbi slices till they are golden
   brown in colour. Drain on absorbent paper. Keep aside.
2. Heat the oil in a non-stick pan and add the ajwain and mustard seeds.
3. When the seeds crackle, add the arbi, turmeric powder, chilli powder,
   coriander powder, lemon juice and salt and mix well.
   Serve hot.

masala tinda

Preparation time :
5 minutes.

Cooking time :
15 minutes.

Serves 2.

This quick and easy vegetable is made using round gourds or tinda tossed with dry spices. Tindas are available for only a short period of time in the year during the monsoons months. They resemble green tomatoes and are firm. Tindas that have a smooth skin are much better to eat than the ones that have a rough fibrous surface.

2 cups tinda (round gourd), cut into half and sliced
½ teaspoon cumin seeds (jeera)
½ teaspoon turmeric powder (haldi)
2 teaspoons chilli powder
2 teaspoons coriander (dhania) powder
2 teaspoons amchur (dry mango powder)
3 tablespoons oil
salt to taste

1. Heat the oil in a non-stick pan and add the cumin seeds.
2. When the seeds crackle, add the tinda and turmeric powder with ¼ cup of water. Cover and cook over a slow flame for about 10 minutes till the tinda is cooked.
3. Add the chilli powder, coriander powder, amchur and salt and mix well.
4. Cook for another 3 to 4 minutes.
   Serve hot.

aloo pethe ka saag

Preparation time :
15 minutes.

Cooking time :
15 minutes.

Serves 6 to 8.

Potatoes and pumpkin (petha) are favourite vegetables of the Rajasthanis and feature in different guises in their cooking.
Potato and pumpkin cooked with whole spices and curds can be relished with plain or stuffed puris.
The addition of fennel gives this vegetable its characteristic Rajasthani flavour.

4½ cups (450 grams) red pumpkin (kaddu), cubed
4½ cups (450 grams) potatoes, cubed

2 bay leaves
12 mm. (½") stick cinnamon
2 cloves
2 cardamoms
1 teaspoon nigella seeds (kalonji)
½ teaspoon mustard seeds (rai)
½ teaspoon fenugreek seeds (methi)
2 tablespoons fresh curds
¼ teaspoon asafoetida (hing)
1 teaspoon chilli powder
2 teaspoons coriander-cumin seed (dhania-jeera) powder
½ teaspoon turmeric powder (haldi)
1 tomato, chopped
1 teaspoon amchur (dry mango powder)
½ teaspoon sugar
3 tablespoons ghee
salt to taste

1. Heat the ghee and fry the bay leaves, cinnamon, cloves, cardamoms, nigella seeds, mustard seeds and fenugreek seeds until the seeds begin to crackle.
2. Add the curds, asafoetida, chilli, coriander-cumin seed and turmeric powders and fry for 2 to 3 minutes.
3. Add the tomato and fry for 1 minute.
4. Add the potatoes, pumpkin and ½ cup of water, cover and cook on a medium heat for 10 to 12 minutes or until the vegetables are tender.
5. Add the amchur powder, sugar and salt.
   Serve hot.

mooli ki subji

Preparation time :
10 minutes.

Cooking time :
15 minutes.

Serves 3.

This is made in the winter when vegetables are easily available. Radish is either chopped or grated to make this dish. If you choose to grate the radish, you do not need to boil it. Remember to chop the radish leaves very finely.

Kachri is a fruit from the melon family which is bitter sweet in flavour. It grows abundantly in the desert region and is rarely cultivated as a crop. Kachri is dried and powdered for use and sent for sale to urban areas where it is not available.

Kachri powder can sometimes be substituted with amchur powder but for this recipe, it is best not to substitute it.

2 medium white radish (mooli), peeled and chopped with the leaves
a pinch soda bi-carb
½ teaspoon cumin seeds (jeera)
½ teaspoon ajwain (carom seeds)
¼ teaspoon asafoetida (hing)
2 teaspoons ginger-green chilli paste
¼ teaspoon turmeric powder (haldi)
2 teaspoons coriander (dhania) powder
1 teaspoon chilli powder
1 tablespoon kachri powder
2 tablespoons oil
salt to taste

1) **Atte ka Malpua**, *page 121*
2) **Methi Mangodi**, *page 45*
3) **Masala Tikadia**, *page 79*
4) **Dal Banjari**, *page 67*

1. Boil the radish (with the leaves) with soda bi-carb in water till it is cooked (approx. 5 to 7 minutes). Drain and keep aside.
2. Heat the oil in a pan, add the cumin seeds, ajwain, asafoetida and ginger-green chilli paste and sauté for a few seconds.
3. Add the cooked radish, turmeric powder, coriander powder, chilli powder, kachri powder and salt. Mix well and sauté for 4 to 5 minutes. Serve hot.

handy tip Use only tender radish leaves for the recipe.

1) **Gavarfali ki Subji,** *page 37*
2) **Bajra Roti,** *page 82*
3) **Aam ki Launji,** *page 96*

ker aur kismis

Preparation time :
15 minutes.

A simple but superbly flavoured dish. Ker (desert berries), sultanas and khoya (mava) are mildly spiced, so as to retain the delicate flavour of the ingredients.

Cooking time :
20 minutes.

Prepare this recipe as close to serving time as possible. Serve hot with bajra or makai rotis.

Serves 2 to 3.

¼ cup ker
¼ cup sultanas (kismis)
2 teaspoons chilli powder
2 tablespoons khoya (mava), grated
1 tablespoon ghee
salt to taste

1. Clean and wash the ker and soak it overnight. Drain and keep aside.
2. Heat the ghee in a pan, add the ker, chilli powder and salt and sauté for 2 minutes.
3. Add ½ cup of water and simmer till the moisture has evaporated and the ker is cooked.
4. Add the sultanas and ½ cup of water and simmer for another 4 to 5 minutes.
5. Add the khoya and mix well.
   Serve hot.

palak mangodi

Preparation time :
15 minutes.

Cooking time :
20 minutes.

Serves 4.

Jodhpuris are extremely fond of moong dal mangodis, which they cook in a variety of ways. Their food includes a lot of greens, so that is perhaps how this combination came about.

Mangodis tossed in a spicy spinach gravy makes a mouth-watering treat.

You can make mangodis very easily at home (see recipe on page 136) or you can buy them in packets from speciality stores. Moong dal mangodis are more common than urad dal mangodis which are made in some parts of Rajasthan.

2 bunches spinach (palak)
1 cup moong dal mangodi, crushed, page 136
2 teaspoons cumin seeds (jeera)
½ cup onions, finely chopped
2 teaspoons ginger-green chilli paste
1 teaspoon garam masala
a pinch turmeric powder (haldi)
1 teaspoon chilli powder
1 tablespoon oil
salt to taste

1. Blanch the spinach in hot water. Wash under a tap of cold water and drain completely.
2. Purée the spinach to a smooth paste in a blender. Keep aside.
3. Combine the mangodi with 2 cups of water and pressure cook for 3 whistles. Drain and keep aside.
4. Heat the oil in a pan and add the cumin seeds. When the seeds crackle, add the onions and sauté till they turn translucent.
5. Add the ginger-green chilli paste and sauté for a few seconds.
6. Add the garam masala, turmeric powder, chilli powder and spinach purée.

7. Lastly, add the cooked mangodis and salt and simmer for 4 to 5 minutes.
Serve hot.

 2 bunches of spinach (palak) will give you approx. 1½ cups spinach purée.

kacher subji

An assortment of vegetables cooked with spices and predominantly flavoured with kachri powder. Kachri is a wild variety of cucumbers. Fresh kachri which resembles a brown yellow small melon grows wildly in the desert areas and is seldom cultivated as a crop.

Fresh kachri is often added to vegetables and even used to make chutney. It is also dried and powdered and the powder, when used in cooking, adds a tangy taste. Since fresh kachri is rarely available outside Rajasthan, the use of kachri powder is popular.

It can also be substituted with 1 teaspoon of amchur in case you cannot find kachri powder.

½ cup carrots, peeled and cubed
½ cup white pumpkin (doodhi or lauki), peeled and cubed
½ cup potato, peeled and cubed
½ cup french beans, diced
½ cup cauliflower, cut into florets
5 cloves garlic, finely chopped
1 teaspoon shah jeera (caraway seeds)
2 teaspoons coriander (dhania) powder
¼ teaspoon turmeric powder (haldi)
1 teaspoon chilli powder
½ cup tomato, diced
1 teaspoon lemon juice
1 tablespoon kachri powder
3 tablespoons oil
salt to taste

For the garnish
2 tablespoons chopped coriander

1. Heat the oil in a non-stick pan, add the garlic and shah jeera and sauté for a few seconds.
2. Add the carrots, white pumpkin, potato, french beans, cauliflower, coriander powder, turmeric powder and chilli powder and mix well.
3. Cover and cook over a slow flame till the vegetables are cooked (approximately 7 to 8 minutes), stirring occasionally.
4. Add the tomato and salt and sauté for another 3 to 4 minutes.
5. Add the lemon juice and kachri powder and mix well.
   Serve hot, garnished with the coriander.

Kadhi aur Dal

****

gatte ki kadhi

Picture on page 26

Preparation time :
20 minutes.

Cooking time :
25 minutes.

Serves 4.

'Gattas' or 'gatte' are gram flour dumplings that are spiced up with dry masalas and then steamed and cut into small bite sized pieces. They are used to make a wide variety of dishes like subji, pulao etc.

This dish is made using a yoghurt based gravy and dry masalas to create a mouth-watering recipe that will complement both rice and parathas.

Another version of the gatte ki kadhi made using an onion and tomato based gravy is usually prepared in the winter when vegetables are easily available.

For the gattas

¾ cup Bengal gram flour (besan)
1 teaspoon chilli powder
1 teaspoon fennel seeds (saunf)
⅛ teaspoon ajwain (carom seeds)
1 tablespoon curds
2 tablespoons oil
salt to taste

For the kadhi

2 cups curds, beaten
1 tablespoon Bengal gram flour (besan)
4 to 6 curry leaves
1 teaspoon cumin seeds (jeera)
½ teaspoon mustard seeds (rai)
½ teaspoon fennel seeds (saunf)
¼ teaspoon asafoetida (hing)
1 bay leaf
1 clove
1 stick cinnamon
1 cardamom (elaichi)
¼ teaspoon turmeric powder (haldi)
2 teaspoons chilli powder

2 teaspoons coriander (dhania) powder
2 tablespoons oil
salt to taste

For the garnish
2 tablespoons chopped coriander

For the gattas

1. Combine all the ingredients for the gattas. Knead into a firm dough using 1 to 2 tablespoons of water.
2. Divide the mixture into 8 equal portions and shape each portion into a 75 mm. (3") long cylindrical roll.
3. Boil plenty of water in a pan and cook the gattas in boiling water for 7 to 8 minutes. Drain.
4. Cut the gattas into 12 mm. (½") long pieces. Keep aside.

For the kadhi

1. Combine the beaten curds, gram flour, ½ cup of water and curry leaves and mix well so that no lumps remain.
2. Heat the oil in a pan, add the cumin seeds, mustard seeds, fennel seeds, asafoetida, bay leaf, clove, cinnamon and cardamom.
3. When the seeds crackle, add the turmeric powder, chilli powder and coriander powder and sauté for a few seconds.
4. Add the curd mixture, 1 cup of water and salt and bring to a boil while stirring continuously, so that the kadhi does not split. Keep aside.

How to proceed
Add the prepared gattas to the kadhi and bring to a boil. Garnish with the chopped coriander.
Serve hot with rice or parathas.

pithore kadhi

Preparation time :
15 minutes.

Cooking time :
15 minutes.

Serves 4.

This kadhi is similar to a pakoda kadhi except that these pakoda like 'pithore' are made differently. The kadhi is tangy because it uses sour curds instead of fresh curds. The Rajasthanis have acquired a taste for sour curds but not many of us can appreciate such a sharp kadhi. You can use fresh curds in place of sour curds.

For the kadhi

2 cups sour curds, beaten
2 tablespoons Bengal gram flour (besan)
a pinch turmeric powder (haldi)
¼ teaspoon fenugreek seeds (methi)
1 teaspoon cumin seeds (jeera)
1 teaspoon mustard seeds (rai)
1 teaspoon green chillies, finely chopped
7 to 8 curry leaves
2 tablespoons ghee
salt to taste

For the pithore

¾ cup Bengal gram flour (besan)
½ teaspoon turmeric powder (haldi)
1 teaspoon chilli powder
4 tablespoons curds
½ teaspoon mustard seeds (rai)
2 teaspoons ghee
salt to taste
oil for deep frying

For the kadhi

1. Combine the curds, gram flour, turmeric powder and salt in a bowl and whisk well. Add 2 cups of water and mix well.
2. Heat the ghee in a pan and add the fenugreek seeds, cumin seeds, mustard seeds, green chillies and curry leaves.
3. When the seeds crackle, add the curd-gram flour mixture and mix well.

4. Bring the kadhi to a boil while stirring continuously. Simmer for 2 to 3 minutes. Keep aside.

For the pithore

1. Combine the gram flour, turmeric powder, chilli powder, curds, salt and ¾ cup of water in a bowl and whisk well.
2. Heat the ghee in a non-stick pan and add the mustard seeds.
3. When the seeds crackle, add the gram flour mixture and sauté for 5 to 6 minutes over a high flame, while stirring continuously till the mixture leaves the sides of the pan.
4. Pour the mixture on a flat plate (thali) of 150 mm. (6") diameter and allow it to set. Cool completely.
5. Cut the pithore into small 25 mm. (1") squares.
6. Deep fry the squares in hot oil till they are golden brown. Drain on absorbent paper. Keep aside.

How to procced

Add the deep fried pithore to the hot kadhi and serve hot with bajra rotis or gatte ka pulao.

mangodi ki kadhi

Preparation time :
10 minutes.

Cooking time :
15 minutes.

Serves 4.

Mangodis are crushed and cooked with tomatoes to make a delectable dish that can be relished with bajra rotis or tikkar.

I am told that when tomatoes are not available, amchur (dry mango) slices are used to add tang to this dish. You can try it too, if you wish.

1 cup moong dal mangodi, crushed, page 136
1 teaspoon cumin seeds (jeera)
¼ teaspoon asafoetida (hing)
1 cup tomatoes, chopped
1½ teaspoons ginger-green chilli paste
¼ teaspoon turmeric powder (haldi)
½ teaspoon chilli powder
1 teaspoon coriander (dhania) powder
1 tablespoon ghee, melted
salt to taste

For the garnish
chopped coriander

1. Heat the ghee in a pressure cooker and add the cumin seeds and asafoetida.
2. When the seeds crackle, add the crushed mangodi and sauté for 2 to 3 minutes.
3. Add the tomatoes, ginger-green chilli paste, turmeric powder, chilli powder, coriander powder and salt with 3 cups of water and pressure cook for 2 whistles.

Serve hot, garnished with coriander.

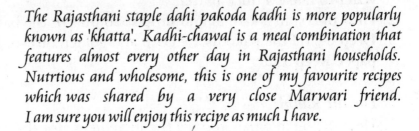

rajasthani kadhi

Picture on page 78

Preparation time :
  15 minutes.

Cooking time :
  30 minutes.

Serves 4.

The Rajasthani staple dahi pakoda kadhi is more popularly known as 'khatta'. Kadhi-chawal is a meal combination that features almost every other day in Rajasthani households. Nutrtious and wholesome, this is one of my favourite recipes which was shared by a very close Marwari friend. I am sure you will enjoy this recipe as much I have.

For the kadhi

4 cups fresh curds, beaten
2 tablespoons Bengal gram flour (besan)
¼ teaspoon turmeric powder (haldi)
salt to taste

For the pakodis

1 cup Bengal gram flour (besan)
2 tablespoons chopped coriander
¼ teaspoon turmeric powder (haldi)
a pinch soda bi-carb
1 teaspoon cumin seeds (jeera)
2 green chillies, finely chopped
salt to taste
oil for deep frying

For the tempering

12 mm. (½") stick cinnamon
2 cloves
2 whole red chillies
½ teaspoon fennel seeds (saunf)
½ teaspoon coriander (dhania) seeds
½ teaspoon cumin seeds (jeera)
¼ teaspoon fenugreek seeds (methi)
2 teaspoons grated ginger
4 to 6 curry leaves
½ teaspon chilli powder
2 tablespoons oil

For the pakodis

1. Mix all the ingredients for the pakodis except the oil and add a little water to make a thick batter.
2. Heat the oil in a kadhai and drop spoonfuls of the batter into the hot oil.
3. Deep fry till the pakodis are crisp and golden brown. Drain on absorbent paper. Keep aside.

For the kadhi

1. Heat the oil in a pan and fry the ingredients for the tempering for 2 minutes. Keep aside.
2. Mix the curds, gram flour, turmeric powder and salt with ½ cup of water and bring to a boil. Pour the tempering over the mixture.
3. Simmer for 10 to 12 minutes.

How to proceed

Add the pakodis to the hot kadhi and mix well. Serve hot.

masala chawla

Preparation time :
20 minutes.

Cooking time :
25 minutes.

Serves 3 to 4.

Lobhia beans are called 'Chawli' in Hindi and that is where this dish gets its name.

Chawli beans are served in a gravy that is flavoured with tomatoes, mint and kasuri methi.

⅓ cup chawli beans (lobhia or black eyed beans)
½ cup onions, finely chopped
2 tomatoes, puréed
¼ teaspoon kasuri methi (dried fenugreek leaves)
¼ teaspoon turmeric powder (haldi)
2 tablespoons oil
salt to taste

To be ground into a paste

¾ cup mint leaves, chopped
1 teaspoon ginger, grated

2 to 3 green chillies

¼ teaspoon lemon juice

1. Clean, wash and soak the chawli beans for at least 2 hours.
2. Pressure cook the chawli beans with water till they are cooked. Drain and keep aside.
3. Heat the oil in a pan, add the onions and sauté till they turn golden brown.
4. Add the puréed tomatoes, kasuri methi, turmeric powder and salt and cook over a slow flame till the oil has separated from the gravy.
5. Add the cooked chawli and ½ cup of water and simmer for 4 to 5 minutes.
6. Add the prepared paste and mix well and cook for another 2 to 3 minutes.
Serve hot.

dal banjari

*Preparation time :
15 minutes.*

*Cooking time :
30 minutes.*

Serves 4 to 6.

A pot of pulses seasoned with simple spices was lit up with firewood and simmered for several hours to make this dal preparation. The cooks would have a meal ready around the time the maharaja returned from shikaar. It would consist of this dal, along with a meat preparation eaten with rotis.

This is a quicker version of the traditional recipe but tastes just as delicious.

1 cup black urad dal (split black lentils with skin)

½ cup split Bengal gram (chana dal)

¼ teaspoon turmeric powder (haldi)

1 onion, sliced

2 cloves

1 stick cinnamon

2 whole red chillies

2 teaspoons ginger-garlic paste

1 teaspoon green chillies, finely chopped

1 teaspoon chilli powder

2 tablespoons ghee

salt to taste

For the garnish
2 tablespoons chopped coriander
ginger, cut into thin strips (julienne)

1. Clean and wash the dals together. Pressure cook with the turmeric powder, salt and 3 cups of water for 4 to 5 whistles or until the dal is cooked.
2. Heat the ghee in a pan, add the onion, cloves, cinnamon and red chillies and sauté till the onion turns golden brown.
3. Add the ginger-garlic paste, green chillies and chilli powder and sauté for 2 minutes.
4. Add this to the cooked dal and boil for 4 to 5 minutes.
   Serve hot, garnished with the coriander and ginger strips.

palak toovar dal

*Preparation time :
20 minutes.*

*Cooking time :
20 minutes.*

Serves 4.

A spicy spinach and lentil preparation that you will enjoy with steamed rice or Khoba Rotis, page 84.

Do not overcook this dal as the spinach tends to discolour quickly.

2 cups spinach (palak), chopped
½ cup toovar (arhar) dal
1 teaspoon ginger, finely chopped
1 teaspoon green chillies, finely chopped
¼ teaspoon turmeric powder (haldi)
½ teaspoon chilli powder
2 tablespoons chopped coriander
salt to taste

For the tempering
3 bay leaves
3 cloves
3 whole red chillies
½ teaspoon cumin seeds (jeera)

a pinch asafoetida (hing)
1 tablespoon ghee

1. Clean, wash and soak the toovar dal for 2 hours. Drain and keep aside.
2. Combine the soaked toovar dal, spinach, ginger, green chillies, turmeric powder, salt and 3 cups of water and pressure cook for 2 whistles.
3. For the tempering, heat the ghee in a pan. Add the bay leaves, cloves, red chillies, cumin seeds and asafoetida.
4. When the seeds crackle, pour the tempering over the cooked dal. Add the chilli powder and chopped coriander, mix well and simmer for 4 to 5 minutes.

Serve hot.

mooli moong dal

Preparation time :
15 minutes.

Cooking time :
20 minutes.

Serves 4.

Mooli or white radish is extensively used in Rajasthani cooking unlike in other parts of India where it's merely considered a salad vegetable.

Radish adds sharp and pungent accents in this bland moong dal. And like all traditional Rajasthani recipes, this dal too, is tempered with ghee.

Some households even add tender radish leaves along with the radish to provide extra flavour to the dal. You can do that too!

½ cup yellow moong dal (split yellow gram)
1 cup white radish (mooli), finely chopped
½ teaspoon turmeric powder (haldi)
½ teaspoon cumin seeds (jeera)
1 bay leaf
2 cloves
2 green chillies, finely chopped
6 mm. (¼") piece ginger, grated
¼ teaspoon asafoetida (hing)
1 teaspoon chilli powder
½ cup chopped coriander

1 tablespoon ghee
salt to taste

1. Clean and wash the dal. Combine the dal, radish, turmeric powder and salt with 2 cups of water and pressure cook till the dal is tender.
2. Heat the ghee in a pan and add the cumin seeds, bay leaf and cloves.
3. When the seeds crackle, add the green chillies, ginger, asafoetida and chilli powder and stir.
4. Add the mixture to the cooked dal and mix well. Simmer for 4 to 5 minutes.
5. Add the chopped coriander and mix well.
   Serve hot.

Roti, Puri aur Paratha

bhedawi puri

Preparation time :
20 minutes.

Cooking time :
30 minutes.

Makes 10 puris.

These puris have a hint of some unusual flavours like urad dal, fennel seeds and kalonji.

Traditionally served with 'sookha aloo' (a dry potato preparation) for breakfast, they can also be served as part of a main meal.

For the dough
1½ cups plain flour (maida)
2 tablespoons hot oil
½ teaspoon nigella seeds (kalonji)
2 pinches salt

For the masala powder (for the stuffing)
1 tablespoon coriander (dhania) seeds
1 tablespoon cumin seeds (jeera)
1 teaspoon fennel seeds (saunf)
8 black peppercorns
4 large or 8 small red chillies

For the stuffing
½ cup urad dal (split black lentils)
2 tablespoons oil
salt to taste

Other ingredients
oil or ghee for deep frying

For the dough
1. Mix all the ingredients and add enough water to make a stiff dough.
2. Knead well and keep aside for 20 minutes.

For the masala powder (for the stuffing)
1. Dry roast the ingredients on a hot tava (griddle) for 1 minute. Cool.
2. Grind into a powder.

For the stuffing

1. Soak the urad dal in water for 4 hours. Drain.
2. Grind coarsely in a blender using very little water.
3. Heat the oil and fry the dal paste until light golden in colour. Cool.
4. Add the masala powder and salt. Mix well.

How to proceed

1. Knead the dough and divide into 10 portions.
2. Roll out each portion of the dough into a thin round of about 50 mm. (2") diameter with the help of a little flour.
3. Put a little stuffing mixture in each round. Close the edges to cover the stuffing completely and roll out again into small puris.
4. Deep fry the puris in hot oil until golden brown. Serve hot.

misi roti

Picture on page 78

*Preparation time :
10 minutes.*

*Cooking time :
15 minutes.*

Makes 8 rotis.

These are a regular part of a Rajasthani meal and sometimes variations are made by adding methi leaves or coriander leaves to flavour the dough.

Misi rotis are eaten throughout the year except in the winters when bajra rotis are preferred.

Serve these with a spicy vegetable or a tongue tickling launji to make a delicious meal.

1 cup whole wheat flour (gehun ka atta)
½ cup Bengal gram flour (besan)
1 teaspoon cumin seeds (jeera)
½ teaspoon ajwain (carom seeds)
a pinch asafoetida (hing)
4 teaspoons melted ghee
salt to taste

Other ingredients
melted ghee for brushing

1. Combine all the ingredients in a bowl and knead into a stiff dough using enough water.
2. Divide the dough into 8 equal portions.
3. Roll out each portion into a 100 mm. (4") diameter circle.
4. Cook the rotis on a hot tava (griddle) until both sides are golden brown.
5. Brush one side of the roti with melted ghee.

Serve hot.

handy tip You can add ¼ cup finely chopped fenugreek leaves (methi) to the above recipe.

bajra aloo roti

Preparation time : 15 minutes.

Cooking time : 15 minutes.

Makes 6 rotis.

Bajra grows abundantly in large parts of arid Rajasthan, especially in the areas around Jodhpur and Dungarpur i.e. Western Rajasthan. Bajra rotis and khichdi are therefore more popular in these areas.

Bajra rotis are preferred in the winter months as bajra is considered to be heat producing.

I have added a little extra flavour to the rotis by the addition of potatoes and spices. You can enjoy these rotis just by themselves smeared with ghee and accompanied with sakhar (i.e. unrefined sugar).

2 cups bajra flour (millet flour)
¾ cup potatoes, boiled and mashed
¼ cup onions, finely chopped
¼ cup fresh coconut, grated (optional)
3 to 4 tablespoons chopped coriander
2 teaspoons ginger-green chilli paste
1 teaspoon amchur (dry mango powder)
½ teaspoon garam masala (optional)
salt to taste

Other ingredients
ghee for cooking

1. Combine all the ingredients to make a soft dough, using warm water.
2. Divide the dough into 6 equal portions and roll out each portion into a 150 mm. (6") diameter circle.
3. Cook the rotis on a hot tava (griddle) using a little ghee, until both sides are golden brown.
   Serve hot.

dal ke parathe

Preparation time :
15 minutes.

Cooking time :
15 minutes.

Makes 6 parathas.

Moong dal is used extensively in Rajasthani cooking from starters like chilas and vadas, to desserts like moong dal halwa etc.

Jodhpuris prefer the use of moong dal to urad dal particularly as it is easier to digest. Thin crispy moong dal parathas complement virtually any Rajasthani subji.

For the dough
¼ cup whole wheat flour (gehun ka atta)
¼ cup plain flour (maida)
2 teaspoons oil
salt to taste

For the filling
½ cup green moong dal (split green gram), soaked for 4 hours
½ teaspoon fennel seeds (saunf)
1 teaspoon chilli powder
a pinch turmeric powder (haldi)
1 tablespoon oil
salt to taste

Other ingredients
oil for cooking

For the dough
1. Combine all the ingredients and knead into a soft dough using enough water. Knead very well.

2. Cover the dough with a wet muslin cloth. Keep aside.

For the filling

1. Wash the dal thoroughly. Drain completely and grind the dal to a fine paste in a blender without using any water.
2. Heat the oil in a non-stick pan, add the dal paste and sauté over a medium flame for 3 to 4 minutes or till the mixture leaves the sides of the pan.
3. Remove from the fire, add the fennel seeds, chilli powder, turmeric powder and salt and mix well.
4. Divide the filling into 6 equal parts. Keep aside.

How to proceed

1. Divide the dough into 6 equal portions and keep aside.
2. Roll out each portion of the dough into a 75 mm. (3") diameter circle.
3. Place a portion of the filling in the centre of the dough circle.
4. Bring together the edges in the centre to seal the filling inside the dough.
5. Roll out the stuffed dough circle into a thin paratha of 150 mm. (6") diameter.
6. Repeat for the remaining filling and dough to make 5 more dal parathas.
7. Cook each dal paratha on a hot tava (griddle) using a little oil till both sides are golden brown.
   Serve hot with ker sangri or curds.

handy tip You can even roll out the dough circles thicker and deep fry them to make puris.

Dal Baati Churma, *page 102*
1) Baati, *page 105*
2) Churma, *page 115*
3) Panchmel Dal, *page 102*

masala tikadia

Picture on page 51

Preparation time :
10 minutes.

Cooking time :
15 minutes.

Makes 5 rotis.

Crisp and spicy whole wheat breads. Tikadias can be plain or stuffed but they have to be crispened over a slow flame. Smear the tikadias with ghee and serve immediately.

1 cup whole wheat flour (gehun ka atta)
salt to taste

Other ingredients
ghee for stuffing and cooking
1 teaspoon roasted cumin seeds (jeera), crushed
1 teaspoon chilli powder

1. Combine the wheat flour and salt and knead into a soft dough using enough water.
2. Divide the dough into 5 equal portions. Keep aside.
3. Roll out each portion of the dough into a circle of 150 mm. (6") diameter.
4. Smear with a little ghee and sprinkle with some cumin seeds and chilli powder.
5. Fold the tikadia and roll up like a Swiss roll. Press a little with your fingers.
6. Roll out each portion into a circle of about 125 mm. (5") diameter.
7. Cook the tikadias on a hot tava (griddle) using a little ghee to cook until both sides are golden brown.
8. Repeat for the remaining dough circles and filling to make 4 more tikadias. Serve hot.

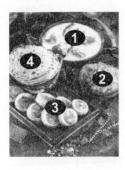

1) **Rajasthani Kadhi,** *page 65*
2) **Badam ka Halwa,** *page 125*
3) **Bharwa Lauki,** *page 41*
4) **Misi Roti,** *page 73*

hare muttar ki puri

Picture on cover

Preparation time :
15 minutes.

Cooking time :
45 minutes.

Makes 12 puris.

Crispy puris stuffed with green peas are superbly flavoured and simply divine. You will enjoy these puris with Aloo ki Subji, page 38. Puris have always been considered a treat for all occasions including the worship of family dieties, birth, naming ceremony of new borns, marriages, housewarming, festivals like Ganesh Pooja, Holi, Teej, Sindhara, Dasshera, Diwali etc.

For the dough
2 cups whole wheat flour (gehun ka atta)
1 tablespoon fresh curds
½ level teaspoon baking powder
1 teaspoon ghee
½ teaspoon salt

For the stuffing
1½ cups boiled green peas
3 to 5 green chillies, finely chopped
1 teaspoon cumin seeds (jeera)
½ teaspoon lemon juice
1 teaspoon chaat masala
1 teaspoon whole wheat flour (gehun ka atta)
1 teaspoon ghee
salt to taste

Other ingredients
ghee or oil for deep frying

For the dough

1. Combine the wheat flour, curds, baking powder, ghee and salt and make a soft dough by adding some warm water.
2. Knead the dough for at least 6 to 7 minutes till it is smooth and elastic.
3. Keep the dough under a wet cloth.
4. Divide the dough into 12 equal portions. Keep aside.

For the stuffing

1. Grind the green peas and green chillies to a paste in a blender, without using any water.
2. Heat the ghee, add the cumin seeds and fry until they crackle.
3. Add the green pea mixture, lemon juice, chaat masala and salt and cook for a few minutes. Sprinkle the flour and cook for 2 to 3 minutes until the mixture becomes dry.

How to proceed

1. Roll out each dough portion into a small round. Put a teaspoon of the stuffing in the centre and close it.
2. Roll out thinly with the help of a little flour. Repeat with the remaining dough portions and stuffing.
3. Deep fry in ghee over a medium flame so that the puris cook from the insides also.
   Serve hot.

bajra roti

Picture on page 52

Preparation time :
5 minutes.

Cooking time :
10 minutes.

Makes 8 rotis.

Though bajra is grown only in certain parts of Rajasthan, bajra rotis are relished all over the state.

Thickly rolled bajra rotis are cooked over 'kanda' (cow dung cakes) in the villages. That is the authentic way of preparing them because it imparts a smoked flavour to the rotis.

Bajra rotis can accompany virtually any vegetable or kadhi on a Rajasthani menu. Bajra roti, lahsun ki chutney and onions is the staple diet of the locals.

Although absolutely simple to make, these rotis are delicious! I love to eat them with fresh white butter.

2 cups bajra flour (millet flour)
¼ cup whole wheat flour (gehun ka atta)
salt to taste

Other ingredients
ghee for brushing

1. Combine the bajra flour, wheat flour and salt and add enough hot water to make a soft dough.
2. Divide the dough into 8 equal portions.
3. Roll out each portion into a thin roti of 150 mm. (6") diameter.
4. Generously dust the rotis with dry bajra flour to make the rolling easier.
5. Cook the rotis on a hot tava (griddle) till both sides are light brown in colour.
6. Brush one side of the roti with melted ghee and serve hot.

mooli makai ki roti

Preparation time :
10 minutes.

Cooking time :
15 minutes.

Makes 6 rotis.

This is the Rajasthani version of 'theplas' with the difference that maize flour is used here instead of wheat flour. The radish adds a nice sharpness to the maize flour. Although these rotis are served at mealtimes, I personally also enjoy them with a hot cup of tea.

1 cup maize flour (makai ka atta)
½ cup grated white radish (mooli)
1 teaspoon ginger-garlic paste
1 teaspoon chilli powder
1 tablespoon oil
salt to taste

Other ingredients
oil or ghee for cooking

1. Combine all the ingredients and knead into a soft dough, using enough hot water.
2. Divide the dough into 6 equal portions.
3. Roll out each portion between two sheets of plastic to a 125 mm. (5") diameter circle.
4. Cook the roti on a hot tava (griddle) till both sides are golden brown, using a little oil.
   Serve hot.

khoba roti

Picture on page 26

Preparation time :
5 minutes.

Cooking time :
20 minutes.

Makes 4 rotis.

This bread truly unravels the mystery of the vast desert expanse. The word 'khoba' means indentation or cavity and that is how these rotis are prepared. They are best cooked in a gas tandoor but an ordinary tava (griddle) over gas will give you equally good results, when cooked over a slow flame. Serve this roti hot, smeared with ghee.

2 cups whole wheat flour (gehun ka atta)
2 teaspoons ghee
salt to taste

Other ingredeints
ghee for serving

1. Combine all the ingredients together and knead into a firm dough using enough water.
2. Divide the dough into 4 equal parts and roll out each portion into a 150 mm. (6") diameter circle.
3. Cook each roti on a tava (griddle) for approx. 2 to 3 minutes and remove onto a plate.
4. Pinch the rotis (as shown in the diagram below) to create indentations.
5. Cook each roti on a tava (griddle) over a slow flame till both sides are golden brown.
   Serve hot with ghee and a vegetable of your choice.

Khichdi aur Pulao

bajra khichdi

Picture on page 103

Preparation time :
10 minutes.

Cooking time :
15 minutes.

Serves 3 to 4.

Although jowar is the cereal that is grown in plenty in the Marwar region, bajra is consumed more. Bajra is ground into a flour to make rotis or is coarsely crushed to make a porridge like khichdi that is eaten with a dollop of ghee or sesame oil in the cold desert winters.

Along with the mandatory ghee or sesame oil, pickle, curds, papad and gur also accompany this khichdi.

⅓ cup whole bajra (millet)
3 tablespoons yellow moong dal (split yellow gram)
1 teaspoon cumin seeds (jeera)
½ teaspoon asafoetida (hing)
2 tablespoons ghee
salt to taste

1. Clean and grind the bajra to a coarse powder in a blender. Keep aside.
2. Wash the ground bajra and moong dal together.
3. Combine the bajra-moong dal mixture and salt with 2 cups of water and pressure cook for 4 whistles or until the bajra is cooked.
4. Heat the ghee in a pan and add the cumin seeds and asafoetida. When the seeds crackle, pour this mixture over the cooked khichdi and mix well.
5. Adjust the consistency of the khichdi at the time of serving by adding ½ cup of hot water if necessary.
   Serve hot with ghee, kadhi or curds.

gatte ka pulao

Preparation time :
15 minutes.

Cooking time :
30 minutes.

Serves 4.

Bengal gram is abundantly used in Rajasthani cooking because it grows in plenty in the arid desert conditions. Besan made from Bengal gram is used to make rotis, gatta, mithai and also as a thickening agent for kadhi (khatta).

Gatte ka pulao is made on festive occasions when plain steamed rice is not served. As vegetables are not available throughout the year, cooked gattas are added to spice up this pulao which is usually served with kadhi (khatta) or plain curds.

For the gattas
1 cup Bengal gram flour (besan)
1 teaspoon chilli powder
1 teaspoon fennel seeds (saunf)
½ teaspoon ajwain (carom seeds)
1 tablespoon curds
2 tablespoons oil
salt to taste

For the pulao
1½ cups cooked long grain rice
1 onion, sliced
1 cardamom (elaichi)
2 cloves
½ teaspoon cumin seeds (jeera)
½ teaspoon mustard seeds (rai)
¼ teaspoon asafoetida (hing)
1 teaspoon chilli powder
½ teaspoon turmeric powder (haldi)
½ teaspoon garam masala
1 tablespoon oil
salt to taste

To be ground into a paste
4 cloves garlic
2 green chillies
50 mm. (2") piece ginger
1 small onion

Other ingredients
oil for deep frying

For the garnish
chopped coriander

For the gattas

1. Combine all the ingredients and knead to make a stiff dough adding a little water, if required.
2. Divide the dough into 8 equal portions and shape each portion into a 100 mm. (4") long and 4 mm. (⅙") diameter cylindrical roll.
3. Boil plenty of water and put the gatta strands in it. Cook for 10 to 12 minutes.
4. When cooked, drain the gattas and keep aside.
5. Cut the gattas into small pieces when cool.
6. Deep fry the gatta pieces in hot oil. Drain on absorbent paper and keep aside.

How to proceed

1. Deep fry the sliced onion in hot oil. Drain on absorbent paper and keep aside.
2. Heat the oil in a pan and add the cardamom, cloves, cumin seeds, mustard seeds and asafoetida.
3. Add the prepared paste and sauté for 4 to 5 minutes.
4. Add the cooked rice, deep fried onion, deep fried gattas, chilli powder, turmeric powder, garam masala and salt and mix well.
   Serve hot, garnished with coriander.

gehun ki bikaneri khichdi

Preparation time :
15 minutes.

Cooking time :
15 minutes.

Serves 4.

Rice is not native to Rajasthan as a result of which wheat, bajra and jowar are the preferred cereals even for making rice like dishes like khichdi, raab etc.

Rajasthanis have invented novel and interesting ways wherein they prepare khichdis out of wheat and bajra instead of from rice.

This recipe probably originated in Bikaner and is therefore named after the city.

A wholesome and nutritious wheat and moong dal khichdi is a meal in itself. Serve it with curds, ghee and a spicy mango pickle to thoroughly enjoy it!

1 cup whole wheat (gehun)
¼ cup yellow moong dal (split yellow gram)
¼ teaspoon cumin seeds (jeera)
2 green chillies, slit
¼ teaspoon asafoetida (hing)
2 tablespoons ghee
salt to taste

1. Clean, wash and soak the wheat overnight. Drain and keep aside.
2. Clean, wash and soak the moong dal for 2 to 3 hours. Drain and keep aside.
3. Grind the wheat to a coarse paste in a blender without using any water.
4. Heat the ghee in a pressure cooker and add the cumin seeds, green chillies and asafoetida.
5. When the seeds crackle, add the ground wheat and moong dal and sauté for 4 to 5 minutes.
6. Add salt and 3½ cups of hot water and pressure cook for 6 to 7 whistles or until the wheat is cooked.
   Serve hot.

Achaar aur Launji

ker ka achaar

Preparation time :
10 minutes.

Cooking time :
5 minutes.

Makes 1¼ cups.

There is only one place in Rajasthan that makes 'fresh ker pickle'. It is a small village in Jhunjhunu district where most of the womenfolk are engaged in making this pickle when these berries are harvested.

As I discovered even after months of searching that fresh ker are not available in Mumbai. I have adapted the recipe and used dried ker to make this flavourful pickle, in which all the ingredients are blended together to create a simple but delicious pickle.

⅓ cup ker
2 tablespoons split mustard seeds (rai na kuria)
1 tablespoon split fenugreek seeds (methi na kuria)
1½ tablespoons chilli powder
1 tablespoon fennel seeds (saunf), crushed
a pinch turmeric powder (haldi)
1 teaspoon amchur (dry mango powder)
¼ teaspoon asafoetida (hing)
½ cup mustard oil
2 teaspoons salt

1. Clean, wash and soak the ker in 1 cup of water for 6 to 8 hours. Drain and keep aside.
2. Heat the mustard oil in a pan till it is very hot. Allow to cool completely.
3. Combine the split mustard seeds, split fenugreek seeds, chilli powder, crushed fennel seeds, turmeric powder, amchur, asafoetida, salt and mustard oil and mix well.
4. Add the ker and mix well. Bottle in a sterilised jar and store in a cool dry place.

note This pickle can be stored for upto a year if kept refrigerated in a clean, dry glass jar.

tamatar ki launji

Preparation time :
5 minutes.

Cooking time :
12 minutes.

Makes ½ cup.

'Launji' is a sweet and sour pickle like dish that is very popular on a Rajasthani table. Every region has its own speciality. This one made with tomatoes is popular mainly in the urban areas as tomatoes are available easily in the cities.

In rural areas, the locals make launji out of sprouted methi seeds, raw mango and they use thick rotis made of jowar, bajra or wheat to mop up these delicious launjis.

1 cup tomatoes, finely chopped
a pinch mustard seeds (rai)
¼ teaspoon cumin seeds (jeera)
¼ teaspoon nigella seeds (kalonji)
¼ teaspoon fennel seeds (saunf)
2 green chillies, broken into large pieces
1 teaspoon coriander (dhania) powder
2 teaspoons chilli powder
1 tablespoon sugar
1 tablespoon chopped coriander
1 tablespoon oil
salt to taste

1. Heat the oil in a pan and add the mustard seeds, cumin seeds, nigella seeds and fennel seeds.
2. When the seeds crackle, add the tomatoes and green chillies and sauté for 2 minutes over a medium flame, while stirring continuously.
3. Add the coriander powder, chilli powder and ¼ cup of water and cook for 5 minutes.
4. Add the sugar, coriander and salt and stir till the sugar has dissolved. Serve hot.

shimla mirch ki launji

Picture on cover

Preparation time :
10 minutes.

Cooking time :
15 minutes.

Makes ½ cup.

A launji is made of a delicate balance of sweet and tangy flavours for which each family has its own recipe. This one came from a friend's home. She preferred to use capsicum instead of methi or tomatoes and the results were lip smacking. The secret of making a good launji is to let all the ingredients simmer over a slow flame so that the flavours mingle together to yield a harmonious whole.

1 cup capsicum (shimla mirch), cut into cubes
½ teaspoon nigella seeds (kalonji)
1 teaspoon fennel seeds (saunf)
1 green chilli, chopped
a pinch turmeric powder (haldi)
2 teaspoons coriander (dhania) powder
½ teaspoon chilli powder
¾ teaspoon amchur (dry mango powder)
2 tablespoons sugar
2 tablespoons oil
salt to taste

1. Heat the oil in a pan, add the nigella seeds, fennel seeds and green chilli and sauté for a minute.
2. Add the capsicum, turmeric powder, coriander powder, chilli powder, salt and ⅓ cup of water and simmer for 4 to 5 minutes till the capsicum is cooked.
3. Add the amchur and sugar and mix well. Cook till the sugar has dissolved.
4. Cool completely. Store refrigerated.
   Serve with bajra rotis.

methi ki launji

Preparation time :
30 minutes.

Cooking time :
20 minutes.

Makes 2 cups.

You will simply adore this launji with rotis, khakhris and even rice although the Rajasthanis would relish it with hot puris or parathas. This bitter-sweet and spicy dish has a delicate balance of flavours that I am sure you will enjoy.

You can either sprout the methi seeds to make this launji or use them unsprouted. I discovered that sprouting the methi makes the launji less bitter.

¼ cup fenugreek seeds (methi)
½ teaspoon cumin seeds (jeera)
¼ teaspoon asafoetida (hing)
½ cup jaggery (gur), grated
½ cup sugar
1 tablespoon amchur (dry mango) slices, finely chopped
2 tablespoons oil
salt to taste

To be mixed together into a masala
3 teaspoons chilli powder
3 teaspoons coriander (dhania) powder
2 teaspoons amchur (dry mango powder)
1 teaspoon turmeric powder (haldi)
1 teaspoon dried dates (kharek), deseeded and chopped
1 tablespoon sultanas (kismis)
½ cup water

1. Soak the fenugreek seeds in 1 cup of water and leave overnight.
2. Next day, drain the fenugreek seeds and add 1 cup of water. Pressure cook for 2 to 3 whistles. Drain and keep aside. Discard the water.
3. Heat the oil in a pan and add the cumin seeds and asafoetida. When the seeds crackle, add the prepared masala, jaggery, sugar, amchur slices and salt and simmer for 5 to 7 minutes. Cool completely.
4. Serve with puris or parathas.
   Store refrigerated for upto 2 weeks.

aam ki launji

Picture on page 52

Preparation time :
5 minutes.

Cooking time :
10 minutes.

Serves 3 to 4.

Raw mangoes are supposed to be 'cooling' for our body system. To beat the intense desert heat, a drink called 'Kairi ka Pani', page 11, is made using raw mango pulp, flavoured with jeera powder, sugar and black salt.

This recipe is another way to combat the heat. Raw mangoes are tempered with fennel and nigella seeds and simmered with spices and sugar to make an instant pickle that can be served with afternoon meals.

1 cup raw mango, peeled and cubed
½ teaspoon fennel seeds (saunf)
¼ teaspoon nigella seeds (kalonji)
3 teaspoons coriander (dhania) powder
1 teaspoon chilli powder
¼ teaspoon turmeric powder (haldi)
⅓ cup sugar
2 tablespoons oil
salt to taste

1. Heat the oil in a pan, add the fennel seeds, nigella seeds and mango pieces and sauté for 2 minutes.
2. Add the coriander powder, chilli powder, turmeric powder, sugar and salt with 4 tablespoons of water. Stir and simmer till the sugar has dissolved.
3. Allow to cool completely.
   Store refrigerated for up to 4 days.

lahsun ki chutney

Preparation time :
5 minutes.

No Cooking.

Makes ¾ cup.

A simple but delectable dry garlic chutney that is a 'must' in every Rajasthani kitchen, whether the king's or a peasant's. This is usually relished with bajra rotis and onions and is part of a peasant's working lunch.

1 cup garlic cloves, peeled
1 tablespoon chilli powder
juice of ½ lemon
salt to taste

1. Combine all the ingredients in a blender with ¼ cup of water and grind to a fine paste.
2. Before using, dilute with water and use as required. Store refrigerated.

amla murabba

Preparation time :
10 minutes.

Cooking time :
1 hour 15 minutes.

Makes 2½ cups.

Maturing time :
2 days.

Storage :
Upto 6 months
(in a cool dry place).

This is an invaluable winter preserve. Amlas (Indian gooseberries) are abundantly available during the winter months. You will find amla trees in several parts of Rajasthan and a large quantity of this fruit is used to make preserves.

Whole amlas simmered in a cardamom and saffron flavoured syrup is one of my personal favourites. There are several traditional recipes for making this murabba. Some soak the amlas in alum (phitkari) overnight whilst others sun-dry amlas. I find it easiest to cook the amlas in boiling water to get rid of all the bitter juices. The entire process takes about 2 to 3 days. First, the amlas are simmered in a thin sugar syrup and left aside for 2 days during which the amlas slowly and gradually soak in the syrup. On the third day, amlas are removed and the syrup is boiled again to a thick honey like consistency. Thereafter the amlas and the flavouring are added. The thick syrup helps in the preservation of the murabba and also complements the sharp and acidic amla taste. I am sure you will enjoy this recipe as much I have enjoyed making it for you.

20 nos. (500 grams) amlas (Indian gooseberries)
2½ cups (500 grams) sugar
¼ teaspoon cardamom (elaichi) powder
a few saffron strands

1. Wash the amlas thoroughly. Prick them with a fork at regular intervals.
2. Boil plenty of water in a pan, add the amlas and boil for 10 minutes over a high flame. Drain and keep aside.
3. Dissolve the sugar in 3 cups of water and bring the syrup to a boil. Add the amlas and cook over a slow flame for about 30 to 40 minutes or until the amlas are soft.

4. Allow the mixture to cool completely. Keep covered in a cool dry place for at least 48 hours so that the amlas soak in the syrup.

5. Drain the amlas from the syrup, boil the syrup with cardamom powder and saffron till it reduces to a 2 to 3 string consistency. Add the amlas and simmer for 3 to 4 minutes.

6. Allow to cool completely.

7. Bottle in a sterilised glass jar. Store for upto 6 months in a cool dry place.

aam aur chane ka achaar

Preparation time :
24 hours.

Cooking time :
2 minutes.

Makes 2 cups.

Maturing time :
6 to 7 days.

Storage :
Upto 1 year
(in a cool dry place).

The summers in Rajasthan are quite unbearable, but they have one saving grace—the mango season. Everyone looks forward to the yearly mango crop and housewives get busy blending the myriad spices needed for a whole year's supply of mango pickles.

This recipe from the Marwar region is of a tongue tickling grated mango and chick pea pickle combined judiciously with whole and powdered spices.

Like all oil pickles, this has a shelf life of upto one year but I am sure it will be eaten up much before that.

½ cup chick peas (kabuli chana)
1½ cups grated raw mango
1 teaspoon turmeric powder (haldi)
1 tablespoon fenugreek seeds (methi)
1 tablespoon fenugreek seeds (methi) powder
1 tablespoon fennel seeds (saunf)
½ teaspoon asafoetida (hing)
1 teaspoon nigella seeds (kalonji)
14 whole red chillies
1 tablespoon chilli powder
1¼ cups mustard oil (sarson ka tel)
1 tablespoon salt

1. Combine the grated mango, turmeric powder and salt and leave aside for 30 minutes. Squeeze out all the mango water. Keep aside the raw mango water and grated mango separately.
2. Soak the fenugreek seeds and chick peas in the mango water overnight.
3. Refrigerate the grated mango.
4. Combine the fenugreek seed powder, fennel seeds, asafoetida, nigella seeds, whole red chillies, chilli powder and soaked chick peas mixture along with the grated mango. Mix well.
5. Heat the mustard oil. Cool it and add to the prepared mixture.
6. Bottle the pickle in a sterilised glass jar.
7. The pickle is ready to eat after 6 to 7 days.
8. Store it a cool dry place for upto 1 year.

Traditional Combinations

dal baati churma

Picture on page 77

Preparation time :
20 minutes.

Cooking time :
1 hour.

Serves 5.

Rajasthani food is incomplete without the mention of the famed Dal-Baati-Churma. What started as a picnic food has become a distinctive cuisine of the State. It consists of baatis or flaky round breads baked over firewood or over kandas (i.e. cow dung cakes) as done in villages. Baatis can be baked in a gas tandoor or an electric oven as well. Bafla or steamed baatis are also very popular.

But one thing common for baatis, irrespective of their cooking technique is that they are always served dipped in ghee accompanied with panchmel or panch kutti dal and churma.

The dal is cooked with ghee, the masalas in the dal are fried in ghee and more ghee is mixed into the dal before serving.

Often a large batch of baatis is made and part of the dough is left unsalted. This unsalted dough then shaped into rounds and deep fried in ghee. Later these deep fried baatis are crushed and sugar or jaggery is mixed into them to make a sweet dessert —Churma.

The three together, simple though they sound, make a very filling meal.

No festive or wedding menu is complete without this popular recipe.

For the panchmel dal

Picture on page 77

⅓ cup split Bengal gram (chana dal)
⅓ cup toovar (arhar) dal
⅓ cup green moong dal (split green gram)

1) Stuffed Dahi Vadas, *page 14*
2) Motichur Laddu, *page 126*
3) Bajra Khichdi, *page 86*

1 tablespoon urad dal (split black lentils)
1 tablespoon whole moong (whole green gram)
3 teaspoons chilli powder
¼ teaspoon turmeric powder (haldi)
1 teaspoon coriander (dhania) powder
½ teaspoon garam masala
3 cloves
2 bay leaves
1 teaspoon cumin seeds (jeera)
2 green chillies, slit
a pinch asafoetida (hing)
2 teaspoons amchur (dry mango powder)
2 teaspoons tamarind (imli) pulp
3 tablespoons ghee
salt to taste

For the baatis (for 10 baatis)   *Picture on page 77*
1 cup whole wheat flour (gehun ka atta)
½ cup semolina (rawa)
2 tablespoons Bengal gram flour (besan)
8 tablespoons milk
4 tablespoons melted ghee
salt to taste

For serving
melted ghee
1 recipe churma, page 115

1) **Makai Jajaria,** *page 130*
3) **Doodhiya Kheech,** *page 132*
4) **Ghevar with Rabdi,** *page 122*

For the panchmel dal

1. Clean and wash the dals and add 4 cups of water. Pressure cook for 2 to 3 whistles or till the dals are cooked.
2. In a bowl, combine the chilli powder, turmeric powder, coriander powder, garam masala with 3 tablespoons of water and mix well. Keep aside.
3. Heat the ghee in a pan and add the cloves, bay leaves, cumin seeds, green chillies and asafoetida. When the cumin seeds crackle, add the prepared masala paste and sauté for 1 to 2 minutes.
4. Add the cooked dal, amchur, tamarind pulp and salt and simmer for 5 to 7 minutes. Adjust the consistency of the dal before serving and if required, add some water.

For the baatis

1. Mix all the ingredients and knead into a firm dough. Knead well for 5 to 7 minutes.
2. Divide the dough into 10 equal portions and shape each portion into an even sized round. Flatten the rounds lightly using your thumb to make an indentation in the centre of the baati.
3. Boil water in a broad vessel and drop the baatis in the boiling water.
4. Cook for 15 to 20 minutes over a high flame.
5. When the baatis are done, drain and keep aside.
6. Heat a gas tandoor and put the baatis on the grill of the tandoor.
7. Cook them on a medium flame for 20 to 25 minutes. Cooking the baatis over a medium flame will ensure that the baatis are cooked on the insides also.
8. Arrange the baatis on a serving plate, break each baati into two pieces and pour melted ghee on the baatis.

How to proceed

Pour hot panchmel dal over the baatis.
Serve hot with churma.

 handy tip You can cook the baatis in a gas tandoor (without boiling them) or bake the boiled baatis in a pre-heated oven at 200°C (400°F) for 10 to 15 minutes turning them over occasionally or even deep fry them in hot ghee instead of cooking them in a tandoor.

masala baati

Preparation time :
10 minutes.

Cooking time :
45 minutes.

Serves 5.

Baati, the famous Rajasthani bread truly unravels the magic and mystique of its cuisine. There are several innovative methods and recipes for making baatis.

This recipe of green pea stuffed whole wheat baatis is one of my personal favourites.

You can use a moong dal (mogar) stuffing instead of this one that I have chosen.

Enjoy these hot baatis immersed in ghee with the famous panchmel dal for a mouth-watering experience.

For the baatis
1 cup whole wheat flour (gehun ka atta)
½ cup semolina (rawa)
4 tablespoons melted ghee
8 tablespoons milk
salt to taste

For the stuffing
1 cup green peas, boiled and crushed
½ teaspoon cumin seeds (jeera)
¼ teaspoon asafoetida (hing)
½ teaspoon ginger-green chilli paste
¼ teaspoon chilli powder
1 teaspoon coriander (dhania) powder
1½ tablespoons oil
salt to taste

For serving
melted ghee
1 recipe panchmel dal, page 102
1 recipe churma, page 115

For the baatis

1. Combine all the ingredients and knead into a firm dough using milk.
2. Knead well for 5 to 7 minutes.
3. Divide the dough into 10 equal parts. Cover with a wet muslin cloth and keep aside.

For the stuffing

1. Heat the oil in a pan, add the cumin seeds and asafoetida.
2. When the seeds crackle, add the green peas, ginger-green chilli paste, chilli powder, coriander powder and salt and sauté for 2 to 3 minutes.
3. Allow to cool completely. Divide the mixture into 10 equal parts. Keep aside.

How to proceed

1. Roll out each portion of the dough into a circle of 37 mm. (1½") diameter.
2. Place one portion of the stuffing mixture in the centre of the rolled dough circle.
3. Surround the stuffing mixture completely with the dough by slowly stretching it over the filling mixture.
4. Seal the ends tightly and remove any excess dough if necessary.
5. Flatten the rounds lightly and make a small indentation in the centre of the baati using your thumb.
6. Boil water in a large pan and drop the baatis into the boiling water. Cook for 15 minutes over a high flame. Drain and keep aside.
7. Heat a gas tandoor and place the baatis on the grill of the tandoor.
8. Cook them over a medium flame for 20 to 25 minutes so that the baatis get cooked on the insides also.
9. Arrange the baatis on a serving dish, break them into pieces and pour some melted ghee over.
10. Serve with hot panchmel dal and churma.

 handy tip You can cook the baatis in a pre-heated oven at 200°C (400°F) for 10 to 15 minutes turning them over occasionally or even deep fry them in hot ghee instead of cooking them in a tandoor.

mogar aur chasni chawal

Preparation time :
30 minutes.

Cooking time :
45 minutes.

Serves 4.

Rajasthani food is chilli hot, and can more than raise the temperature of your body!

I presume that is the reason why Rajasthanis are so fond of eating sweets which take the bite off anything that is spicy.

Mogar and chasni chawal is one such fine example, where spicy moong dal or mogar is eaten along with chasni or sweetened rice. The fiery dal is offset by the sweetness in the rice.

These two recipes are therefore always savoured together and never eaten by themselves.

The term 'Mogar' is also used for deep fried moong dal, a snack which available at most 'namkeen' shops in Rajasthan.

For the chasni chawal

1 cup long grained rice
a few drops saffron food colour
½ cup sugar
10 cloves
6 cardamoms (elaichi)
2 tablespoons ghee

For the mogar

1 cup yellow moong dal (split yellow gram)
1 teaspoon cumin seeds (jeera)
¼ teaspoon amchur (dry mango powder)
1 teaspoon chilli powder
¼ teaspoon turmeric powder (haldi)
2 tablespoons chopped coriander
2 tablespoons oil
salt to taste

For the chasni chawal

1. Clean, wash and soak the rice for 10 minutes. Drain and keep aside.
2. Cook the rice with the saffron colour. Drain and keep aside.

3. Combine the sugar with ½ cup of water and make a syrup of one-string consistency. Keep aside.
4. Heat the ghee in a pan, add the cloves and cardamoms and stir for a few seconds.
5. Add the cooked rice and sauté for 2 minutes.
6. Add the syrup to the rice and bring to a boil, while stirring occasionally, till the liquid evaporates.

For the mogar

1. Soak the yellow moong dal for 30 minutes. Drain out all the water.
2. Cook the soaked moong dal with 1½ cups of water till it is cooked but the dal is separate and not mashed. Drain and keep aside.
3. Heat the oil in a pan and add the cumin seeds. When the seeds crackle, add the cooked moong dal, amchur, chilli powder, turmeric powder, chopped coriander and salt. Mix well.
Serve hot with the chasni chawal.

chana dal aur gur chawal

Preparation time :
30 minutes.

Cooking time :
35 minutes.

Serves 3 to 4.

This is another classic combination similar to Mogar and Chasni Chawal.

Dry spicy Bengal gram is necessarily accompanied by this fennel flavoured aromatic jaggery rice.

Rituals and festivals have been always celebrated in a grand way in the true Hindu tradition prevalant all over Rajasthan. Festive foods therefore receive the utmost attention.

Yellow sweetened rice (sweetened with either sugar or jaggery) is always prepared as an offering to Goddess Saraswati on Basant Panchami. A tradition that has been followed by the maharajas through centuries.

For the chana dal

½ cup split Bengal gram (chana dal)
½ teaspoon cumin seeds (jeera)
a pinch asafoetida (hing)
1 teaspoon ginger-green chilli paste
¼ teaspoon turmeric powder (haldi)

1 teaspoon chilli powder
1 teaspoon coriander (dhania) powder
¼ teaspoon black salt (sanchal)
1½ teaspoons lemon juice
2 tablespoons chopped coriander
2 tablespoons oil
salt to taste

For the gur chawal
½ cup long grain rice
2 teaspoons fennel seeds (saunf)
2 cardamoms (elaichi)
½ cup jaggery (gur), grated
1 tablespoon ghee

For the chana dal
1. Clean, wash and soak the chana dal for 3 to 4 hours. Drain and keep aside.
2. Heat the oil in a pan, add the cumin seeds, asafoetida and ginger-green chilli paste and sauté for a few seconds.
3. Add the chana dal, turmeric powder, chilli powder, coriander powder, black salt, lemon juice and salt. Mix well and cook for another 2 minutes.
4. Add 4 tablespoons of water and simmer till all the moisture has evaporated. Add the coriander and mix well.

For the gur chawal
1. Clean, wash and soak the rice for 10 minutes. Drain and keep aside.
2. Heat the ghee in a pan, add the fennel seeds, cardamoms and rice and sauté for 2 to 3 minutes.
3. Add 1½ cups of hot water, cover and cook over a slow flame till the rice is cooked.
4. Add the jaggery and ½ cup of water and simmer while stirring occasionally till the jaggery has dissolved.
   Serve hot with the chana dal.

raabdi with bajra roti

Preparation time :
5 minutes.

Cooking time :
10 minutes.

Serves 3 to 4.

'Raabdi' or 'Raab' as it is commonly known, is a thick gruel prepared using bajre ka atta and curds or buttermilk. Raabdi can be served hot or cold.

It is often eaten as a substitute for rice and is served with chaas (buttermilk) or milk.

An earthenware pot full of bajra flour and buttermilk is often left to simmer over a slow flame in the mornings and it is ready to serve around lunch time after it has simmered for several hours. It does not require a lot of attention, so housewives can complete their other household chores while the raabdi is being cooked.

In some households, raabdi left over from the previous day is often served with hot bajra rotis for breakfast the following day.

¼ cup bajra flour (millet flour)
½ cup curds, beaten
1 tablespoon chopped coriander
a pinch asafoetida (hing)
½ teaspoon ghee
salt to taste

For serving
2 tablespoons curds, beaten
bajra rotis, page 82

1. Combine the bajra flour, curds and salt with 2 cups of water and mix well.
2. Heat the ghee and add the asafoetida. Add this tempering to the bajra mixture.
3. Bring the mixture to a boil while stirring continuously. Simmer for 3 to 4 minutes.
4. Allow it to cool completely.
5. Mix in the remaining curds and chopped coriander and serve with bajra rotis.

Manpasand Mithai

gaund ke laddu

Preparation time :
15 minutes.

Cooking time :
30 minutes.

Makes 15 laddus.

Gaund is an 'edible gum' that is extracted from the bark of a tree. It is available in crystal form as pearly yellowish translucent pieces of varying sizes. The bigger crystals are more expensive. Gaund is a 'heaty' food i.e. food that provides heat to our body and is usually had only in the winters. It is deep fried in ghee and then added to the dish it is being used in. I have also discovered that if you dry roast it on a non-stick pan, it puffs up just like popcorn. This is a great way to cut down on those unnecessary calories. These delicious gaund laddus are a traditional winter delicacy that are had with a glass of warm milk for breakfast. I personally prefer them as a dessert after a nice meal.

1¼ cups whole wheat flour (gehun ka atta)
3 tablespoons gaund (edible gum)
½ cup powdered sugar
½ teaspoon cardamom (elaichi) powder
¼ cup ghee

Other ingredients
ghee for deep frying

1. Heat the ghee in a pan, add the whole wheat flour and roast it over a slow flame while stirring continuously till the flour turns golden brown. Allow it to cool.
2. Deep fry the gaund in hot ghee, one tablespoon at a time till the pieces puff up. Drain on absorbent paper and keep aside.
3. Add the powdered sugar, fried gaund and cardamom powder to the roasted wheat flour and mix well.
4. Divide the mixture into 15 portions and shape each portion into round laddus using your hands. If you find it difficult to shape the laddus, add a little melted ghee.
Store in an air-tight container.

churma

Picture on page 77

Preparation time :
15 minutes.

Cooking time :
20 minutes.

Serves 4 to 6.

Dal-baati is incomplete without the quintessential 'Churma'. Churma is made using coarsely ground wheat flour, besan or maize flour.

The most celebrated of all is the wheat flour churma that can be shaped into laddus. I discovered that the more ghee you add to the churma mixture, the easier it is to shape these laddus. If you use ghee sparingly as we have done in this recipe, you will need to use a lot more pressure to shape them. You can also serve the churma crumbled in which case, you do not need to make laddus.

I have also used rava in this recipe as I realised that it is sometimes difficult to find coarsely ground wheat flour easily. The rava adds that extra bite to the churma, greatly improving the texture of the whole wheat flour.

1 cup whole wheat flour (gehun ka atta)
¼ cup semolina (rawa)
6 almonds, sliced
¼ teaspoon cardamom (elaichi) powder
⅓ cup powdered sugar
4 tablespoons melted ghee

Other ingredients
ghee for deep frying

1. Combine the wheat flour, semolina and 4 tablespoons of melted ghee in a bowl and mix well. Add approx. ¼ cup of water and knead well to make a stiff dough.
2. Divide the dough into 8 equal portions.
3. Shape each dough portion in the shape of your fist and press with your fingers in the centre of each portion to make an indentation (as shown in the diagram below).
4. Heat the ghee in a kadhai and deep fry the dough portions on a very slow flame until they are golden brown in colour. These will take a

long time to fry as the insides need to be cooked also.

5. Drain on absorbent paper and allow them to cool.
6. Grind the fried dough pieces in a blender into a fine powder.
7. Add the almonds, cardamom powder and powdered sugar and mix well.
8. Store in an air-tight container.
   Serve with dal-baati.

VARIATION : *churma laddu*

Add 5 tablespoons of hot ghee to the churma, divide the mixture into 10 portions and shape into laddus.

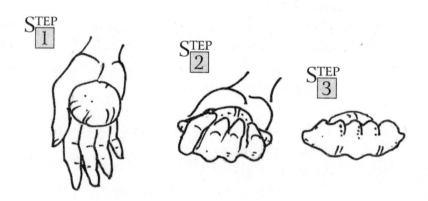

jaripalla churma

Preparation time :
20 minutes.

Cooking time :
35 minutes.

Serves 6.

Jaripalla churma is a richer version of the regular churma. Some also say that it is the 'Marwari' version of churma because it contains expensive ingredients like dry fruits and khoya.

This churma is made for special occasions like weddings and festivals like Janmashtami when it is offered to Lord Krishna. Krishna's love for milk and milk products like makhan and khoya are legendary, so this makes a befitting 'prasad' to him.

For the churma
½ cup whole wheat flour (gehun ka atta)
⅓ cup Bengal gram flour (besan)
2 tablespoons semolina (rawa)
1½ tablespoons melted ghee
ghee for deep frying

Other ingredients
1 cup (150 grams) khoya (mava)
a few drops saffron food colour
½ cup castor sugar or powdered sugar
¼ cup gaund (edible gum)
6 almonds, sliced
6 pistachios, sliced
2 tablespoons misri (khadi sakar) (optional)
½ teaspoon cardamom (elaichi) powder
a few saffron strands
2 tablespoons melted ghee

For the churma
1. Make a stiff dough using wheat flour, gram flour, semolina and 1½ tablespoons of ghee and enough water. Knead very well.
2. Divide the dough into 8 equal portions.

3. Shape the dough portions into the shape of your fist and press with your fingers in the centre of each portion to make an indentation (as shown in the diagram on page 116).
4. Heat ghee in a large kadhai and deep fry the dough portions on a very slow flame for approximately 15 to 20 minutes until they are golden brown in colour.
5. Drain on absorbent paper and allow to cool.
6. Pound the fried dough pieces in a mortar and pestle to get coarse pieces.
7. Grind the pieces further in a blender to get a fine powder (churma).

How to proceed

1. Sauté the mava over a very slow flame along with the saffron food colour for 5 to 7 minutes, while stirring continuously. Allow to cool completely. Grate and keep aside.
2. Deep fry the gaund in hot ghee. Drain an absorbent paper and keep aside.
3. Add the castor sugar, deep fried gaund, grated mava, almonds, pistachios, misri, cardamom powder, 2 tablespoons of melted ghee and a few strands of saffron to the churma. Mix very well. Store in an air-tight container.
   Serve with Dal-Baati.

chenna malpua

Preparation time :
20 minutes.

Cooking time :
30 minutes.

Makes 10 malpuas.

Delicate and lacy malpuas made using fresh paneer which will melt in your mouth. This recipe is somewhat comparable to the famous malai malpuas of Pushkar near Ajmer.

Serve them warm topped with rabdi or just garnished with chopped almonds and pistachios. You will find chenna malpuas only at a few cities in Rajasthan. Just grab the opportunity to make them as they are simply divine!

These malpuas are a little tricky to make, so be patient. Sometimes, they can just disintegrate in the ghee while frying. If that happens, add some more cornflour to bind the dough.

For the chenna
1 litre milk
½ teaspoon citric acid

For the malpuas
1 cup chenna (recipe above)
1 pinch nutmeg (jaiphal) powder
1½ tablespoons cornflour
a few saffron strands

For the sugar syrup
1¼ cups (250 grams) sugar

Other ingredients
ghee for deep frying

For the chenna
1. Dissolve the citric acid in ½ cup of water and keep aside.
2. Bring the milk to a boil in a pan, stirring continuously.
3. Remove from the fire and stir for 5 to 7 minutes till the milk is slightly cool.
4. Add the citric acid solution and stir the milk gently.
5. The milk will curdle and the whey will separate. The whey has to be

clear thus indicating the milk has completely curdled. Allow it to rest for 3 to 4 minutes.

6. Strain out all the whey using a clean damp muslin cloth.
7. Fold all the 4 sides of the muslin cloth and twirl it gently so that the whey that is in the milk solids gets evenly drained out.
8. Gather the cloth from all 4 sides and squeeze the chenna lightly about 3 to 4 times so that most of the whey gets drained out.
9. Remove the chenna onto a clean plate and knead gently so that it is free of lumps, taking care not to apply too much pressure while kneading the chenna.

It is advisable to use this almost immediately.

For the sugar syrup

Dissolve the sugar in 1 cup of water and boil for 5 minutes to get a syrup of 1 string consistency. Keep aside.

For the malpuas

1. Mix the chenna, nutmeg powder, cornflour and saffron into a dough.
2. Divide the dough into 10 equal portions. Place one portion of the dough on a wet muslin cloth and flatten it with wet hands.
3. Heat ghee in a shallow kadhai (the ghee should be approximately 25 mm. (1") deep) and deep fry the malpuas until golden brown in colour.
4. Repeat for the remaining dough.

How to proceed

1. Drain and soak the hot malpuas into the prepared sugar syrup. Allow them to soak for approximately 5 minutes.
2. Drain the malpuas from the syrup and arrange them on a serving plate. Serve warm.

Points to remember for the chenna:

1. Make sure that the milk is lukewarm while adding the citric acid mixture.
2. Do not shock hot milk as it will affect the quality of the chenna.
3. Always use cow's milk for making chenna as it has a low fat content. If you use buffalo's milk, let the milk rest after boiling it and then discard the skin that is formed.

atte ka malpua

Picture on page 51

Preparation time :
15 minutes.

Cooking time :
30 minutes.

Makes 20 malpuas.

Malpuas are rich, soft filigreed pancakes. The pancake (malpua) batter can be sweetened as in this recipe or the fried malpuas can be soaked in a saffron flavoured syrup.

Udaipur and Pushkar are famous for their scrumptious atte ka malpuas. Coarsely ground wheat flour is used in this recipe as it helps to make crisper malpuas. These malpuas are a special feature at festivities and are always prepared for Teej and Hariali Umavas as a sacred offering to please the gods and goddesses.

1 cup coarsely ground whole wheat flour (gehun ka atta)
½ cup sugar
1 tablespoon fennel seeds (saunf)
10 peppecorns, crushed
¼ cup curds, beaten
½ cup milk

Other ingredients
ghee for deep frying

For the garnish
2 teaspoons chopped pistachios

1. Combine all the ingredients in a bowl and add approx. 1½ cups of warm water. Mix well to make a smooth batter. Leave aside for 45 minutes.
2. Heat ghee in a shallow kadhai (the ghee should be approximately 25 mm. (1") deep).
3. Pour a spoonful of the batter into the hot ghee and deep fry over a medium flame. Cook on both sides till the malpua is golden brown.
4. Drain on absorbent paper.

5. Repeat steps 3 and 4 for the remaining batter.
   Serve hot, garnished with pistachios.

handy tip
You will find coarsely ground wheat flour at some provision stores. You can use 2 tablespoons of semolina with 1 cup whole wheat flour (gehun ka atta) instead of coarsely ground wheat flour for the above recipe.

ghevar with rabdi

Picture on page 104

Preparation time :
10 minutes.

Cooking time :
2 hours.

Makes 25 ghevars.

A honeycomb shaped delicacy made using plain flour and ghee that has originated in Rajasthan. Ghevars are usually large in size approx. 200 mm. or 250 mm. (8" or 10") squares or rounds and are either sweetened with syrup or served topped with sweet rabdi (i.e. thickened milk).

Lakshmi Mishtaan Bhandar in Jaipur is famous for their 'melt in the mouth' ghevars and many other sweet shops in Rajasthan also specialise in the same.

Ghevars are earmarked as a traditional dish for some special rituals and festivals. They are generally prepared in January for Makar Sankranti, in March-April for Gangaur and in July-August for the Teej festival.

But you can enjoy these at any time of the year by just following the recipe given below.

For the ghevar
1¾ cups (200 grams) plain flour (maida)
1 tablespoon (10 grams) arrowroot or cornflour
¼ cup melted ghee, slightly cooled
a few drops of kewda essence

For the sugar syrup
1 cup (200 grams) sugar
½ cup water

For the rabdi
½ litre full fat milk
1 tablespoon sugar
a few saffron strands

Other ingredients
ghee for deep frying

For the garnish
chopped pistachios

For the ghevar
1. Combine the flour, arrowroot, kewda essence and melted ghee in a bowl.
2. Add 1 cup of water in a thin stream, whisking continuously taking care to see that an emulsion is formed and the water and ghee do not separate.
3. Add 2 more cups of water again in a thin stream while whisking continuously. At no point should the ghee and water separate.
4. The batter should be of a coating consistency. More water can be added if required to achieve the required consistency.
5. Keep the batter in a cool place away from heat.
6. Place the ghevar mould in a kadhai containing melted ghee upto ¾ of the height of the mould.
7. Remove 2 ladlefuls of the batter at a time into a small bowl and place it near the gas range. Keep the rest of the batter away from heat.
8. Heat the ghee in the kadhai on a medium flame and pour one spoonful of the batter into the centre of the mould in a thin stream. The batter should settle in the mould.
9. When the froth subsides, pour in another spoonful of the batter in the centre of the mould in a thin stream.
10. Repeat seven times making a hole in the centre of the ghevar using a wooden skewer stick. Pour the batter into this centre each time.
11. Increase the flame and allow it to cook in the centre by pouring ladlefuls of hot ghee in the centre of the mould 2 or 3 times.
12. When the centre is firm and cooked, pull the ghevar out gently, by inserting a wooden skewer in the centre and pulling it out of the ghee.

13. Place on a serving plate, immerse in sugar syrup and drain quickly.
14. Repeat steps 7 to 13 and use the remaining batter to make 25 ghevars.

For the sugar syrup

1. Combine the sugar and water in a pan and simmer till it reaches a 1 string consistency.
2. Remove from the heat and keep warm.

For the rabdi

1. Heat the milk in a broad non-stick pan and keep stirring over low heat till it is reduced to one-third.
2. Add the sugar and saffron strands and simmer till the sugar has dissolved.

How to proceed

Serve the ghevars topped with a spoonful of the rabdi.
Garnish with chopped pistachios.

handy tip You have to buy a special ghevar mould to make this delicacy. You can also use a primus stove ring of size 4 (75 mm. (3") in diameter) to obtain 25 ghevars. Alternatively, you can use a larger mould to get fewer ghevars in which case the cooking time will increase.

moong dal halwa

Preparation time :
  10 minutes.

Cooking time :
  40 minutes.

Serves 4 to 6.

A classic recipe that is relished throughout Rajasthan. This calorie laden halwa is often prepared during the winter months, as it is supposed to keep the body warm and protect it from the bitter winter cold. It is considered to be auspicious for Holi and Diwali and it even features on wedding menus.

It takes a long time and a lot of patience to sauté the dal and prepare this halwa and it will probably require a little extra ghee too. You can make a larger quantity of this recipe and store it refrigerated for several weeks. Just add a little milk to the halwa before reheating it.

1 cup yellow moong dal (split yellow gram)
1 cup milk, warmed
1¼ cups sugar
½ teaspoon cardamom (elaichi) powder
a few saffron strands
6 tablespoons ghee

For the garnish
2 tablespoons almonds and pistachios, sliced

1. Soak the moong dal in water for 3 to 4 hours.
2. Drain and grind to a coarse paste using very little water.
3. Dissolve the saffron in 1 tablespoon of warm milk and keep aside.
4. Melt the ghee in a broad non-stick pan.
5. Add the moong dal paste and stir the mixture continuously on a low flame till it becomes golden brown.
6. Add in the warm milk and 1 cup of warm water and cook, stirring continuously till all the moisture has been absorbed.
7. Add the sugar and cook on a slow flame till the ghee separates.
8. Add the saffron and cardamom powder and mix well.
9. Garnish with slivers of almonds and pistachios. Serve hot.

handy tip If the moong dal paste has excess water after grinding, drain it out through a strainer.

badam ka halwa *Picture on page 78*

Preparation time :
15 minutes.

Cooking time :
30 minutes.

Makes approx.
1 cup.

Ever since my childhood, I have been encouraged to have a tablespoon of this halwa every morning in the winters. I used to look forward to winters because of this morning ritual.
This is a rich recipe and one can't have too much of it at one time —but it is delicious nevertheless. It has been my all time favourite winter recipe.

½ cup almonds, soaked overnight
⅓ cup milk

4 tablespoons sugar
¼ teaspoon cardamom (elaichi) powder
3 tablespoons ghee

For the garnish
2 to 3 almonds, peeled and sliced

1. Pour 1 cup of boiling water over the almonds. Leave aside for 5 minutes.
2. Drain and remove the skins of the almonds.
3. Purée the almonds with 4 tablespoons of milk to a smooth paste in a blender.
4. Heat the ghee in a non-stick kadhai and add the almond purée. Cook over a slow flame while stirring continuously till the mixture turns golden brown (approx. 15 minutes).
5. Boil together the remaining milk with 4 tablespoons of water, add to the almond mixture and cook for 2 to 3 minutes.
6. Add the sugar and cardamom powder and cook till the sugar has dissolved, while stirring continuously.
   Serve hot, garnished with the almonds.

motichur laddu   *Picture on page 103*

Preparation time :
20 minutes.

Cooking time :
45 minutes.

Makes 20 to 22 laddus.

Laddus are considered a very auspicious mithai as they are Lord Ganesh's favourite. In Rajasthan, the most popular kinds are the malai laddu, bundi laddu and motichur laddu.

The difference between motichur and bundi laddus is that the bundis in the bundi laddus are larger and are fried till they are slightly brown in colour. Motichur laddus however are made with very small sized bundi, almost like little rice pearls and they are not fried till they darken.

Making these laddus is a time consuming process and a little practice is required to perfect them. If you are patient and enjoy the pursuit, you will enjoy making these 'pearly laddus'.

For the bundi batter
1½ cups Bengal gram flour (besan)
1½ tablespoons semolina (rawa)

For the sugar syrup
1¼ cups (250 grams) sugar
1 tablespoon milk
a few drops saffron food colour

Other ingredients
a few saffron strands
2 tablespoons almonds, chopped
2 tablespoons pistachios, chopped
1 teaspoon cardamom (elaichi) powder
2 teaspoons rose water
ghee for deep frying

For the garnish
silver varq (edible silver sheets) (optional)

For the bundi batter
1. Combine the gram flour, semolina and approx. ¾ cup of water and mix well to make a smooth batter. Keep aside.

For the sugar syrup
1. Combine the sugar and milk with 1½ cups of water in a kadhai and heat while stirring continuously till the sugar dissolves. When the syrup comes to a boil, the impurities in the sugar will begin to float on the surface, forming a grey layer.
2. Heat over a medium flame to allow the grey layer to float. Do not stir at this point as the layer will break and it will not clarify the syrup.
3. After about 5 minutes, slowly drizzle 2 tablespoons of water from the sides of the pan with the help of a ladle. Water added at this stage will bring down the temperature of the sugar syrup and will not allow it to boil and break the grey layer.
4. Continue to simmer the syrup over a medium flame for about 3 to 4 minutes and then gently remove the grey layer using a slotted spoon.
5. Add the saffron food colour to the syrup and make a syrup of one string consistency. Keep warm.

How to proceed

1. Heat ghee in a kadhai. When hot, hold a perforated spoon (bundi jhara) over the hot ghee and pour a little bundi batter at a time using a ladle over the perforated spoon. Spread the batter with the back of a spoon so that the bundi falls into the ghee.
2. Fry the bundis over a high flame to a light golden colour, taking care to ensure that they are not very crisp.
3. Add the bundis to the warm sugar syrup and mix well so that the bundis soak in the syrup well.
4. Wash and dry the perforated spoon (bundi jhara) every time you pour the bundi batter through it. Proceed making the bundis with the remaining batter and immerse them in the sugar syrup immediately after frying.
5. Allow the mixture to cool completely.
6. Add 2 tablespoons of hot water, the saffron, chopped almonds, chopped pistachios, powdered cardamom and rose water and mix well.
7. Shape the mixture to make 20 to 22 laddus and garnish with silver varq, if using.

handy tip Perforated spoons are available in the market especially used for making bundis called 'bundi jharas'.

dilkushar

Preparation time :
10 minutes.

Cooking time :
1 hour.

Makes approx.
20 pieces.

This divine mithai is also called 'Besan ki Chakki' or 'Mohanthal'. This is usually made at weddings and on special occasions.

It is a complicated mithai to make and one needs a little practice to perfect this recipe.

It is traditionally made with coarsely ground besan, so that the barfi has a nice chewy texture, but since it is difficult to obtain coarsely ground besan, you can also use plain besan instead.

2 cups coarsely ground Bengal gram flour (besan)
1 cup ghee
1 cup (150 grams) grated khoya (mava)
1 teaspoon cardamom powder (elaichi)

For the sugar syrup
1½ cups (300 grams) sugar
1 cup water
2 tablespoons milk

For the garnish
4 tablespoons chopped almonds and pistachios

1. Place the gram flour in a bowl.
2. Heat the ghee and pour half of it over the gram flour.
3. Rub the ghee into the gram flour till the mixture resembles bread crumbs.
4. Put the remaining hot ghee in a kadhai, add the gram flour mixture and cook till the mixture is golden brown, stirring continuously.
5. Add the grated khoya and cardamom powder and stir for about 5 to 7 minutes.
6. Remove from the heat and allow to cool till it is warm.

For the sugar syrup
1. Mix the sugar with water in a pan and simmer for 10 minutes.
2. Add the milk to the boiling sugar syrup.
3. The impurities will form a grey layer. Remove this layer gently using a slotted spoon.
4. Simmer till the syrup is of 1 string consistency. Keep the syrup hot.

How to proceed
1. Pour the hot sugar syrup over the cooked gram flour mixture and stir well.
2. Pour into a greased 225 mm. (9") diameter thali with 25 mm. (1") high sides.
3. Sprinkle chopped almonds and pistachios on top and allow to set for 4 to 5 hours.
4. Cut into 25 mm. (1") squares.
   Serve at room temperature.

 handy tip To test if the sugar syrup has reached a 1 string consistency, lift some with a spoon and let it trickle down. If the syrup is dense and leaves a threadlike trail, it is ready to be used.

Preparation time :
10 minutes.

Cooking time :
20 minutes.

Serves 4.

This is a very popular halwa eaten in and around the areas surrounding Udaipur. Here corn is extensively cultivated especially white corn while yellow or sweet corn is grown at a few places.

I prefer the taste of sweet corn in this recipe as compared to white corn but you can use either. This halwa is simple to prepare and superbly flavoured.

2 nos. sweet corn cobs, grated
1 cup milk
½ cup sugar
¼ teaspoon cardamom (elaichi) powder
2 tablespoons ghee

For the garnish
4 corn leaves
4 pistachios, sliced

1. Heat the ghee in a non-stick pan, add the grated corn and cook over a slow flame for 10 to 12 minutes while stirring continuously till the mixture turns light brown in colour.
2. Add the milk and 1 cup of water and simmer till the liquid has evaporated, stirring occasionally.
3. Add the sugar and cardamom powder, mix well and cook till the sugar has dissolved.
4. Serve hot on 4 corn leaves as shown in the picture on page 104, garnished with the sliced pistachios.

bundi payas

An interesting version of kheer in which sweet bundis are used to thicken and flavour the milk.

It is important to remember to cool the milk completely before you add the bundi so that the bundi stays whole. If you add it into hot or warm milk, it is sure to disintegrate giving you a besan flavoured rabdi.

¾ cup sweet bundi, see below
1 litre full fat milk
3 bay leaves
⅓ cup sugar
2 drops saffron food colour
½ teaspoon rose water
1 teaspoon cardamom (elaichi) powder
1 teaspoon pistachios, chopped

1. Heat the milk in a pan along with the bay leaves and reduce it to half its original quantity. Remove the bay leaves and discard them.
2. Add the sugar and mix well till it has dissolved. Allow to cool completely.
3. Add the bundi, saffron food colour, rose water, cardamom powder, pistachios and mix gently.
4. Refrigerate for 2 to 3 hours and serve chilled.

handy tip You can buy sweet bundi, which is available at sweetmeat shops, or make it at home by following the recipe of motichur laddu on page 126.

doodhiya kheech

Picture on page 104

Preparation time :
15 minutes.

Cooking time :
25 minutes.

Serves 3 to 4.

This dish is very popular in Udaipur from where it is said to have originated.

Its texture is similar to that of rabdi although wheat is used to thicken this dessert.

'Kheech' refers to a 'mashed texture' that is almost like porridge. As wheat and milk are rejuvenating foods that provide plenty of energy, it is also served to convalescents who are recovering.

½ cup whole wheat (gehun)
⅓ cup sugar
3 cups full fat milk
a few saffron strands
1 teaspoon cardamom (elaichi) powder
1 tablespoon sultanas (kismis)
1 tablespoon almonds, sliced

1. Clean, wash and soak the wheat overnight.
2. Drain and grind the wheat to a coarse paste in a blender without using any water.
3. Pressure cook the wheat with 1 cup of milk and ½ cup of water for 6 whistles or till the wheat is cooked.
4. Heat the remaining 2 cups of milk with the sugar and saffron and cook till it is reduced to half of its original quantity.
5. Add the cooked wheat to the reduced milk and mix well. Simmer for 5 minutes.
6. Add the cardamom powder, sultanas and almonds and serve hot.

mava kachori

Picture on cover

Preparation time :
15 minutes.

Cooking time :
30 minutes.

Makes 6 kachoris.

Jodhpur is famous for its mava kachoris. Rich dry fruit and mava (khoya) stuffed crisp deep fried kachoris are coated coated in sugar syrup. These kachoris are a welcome treat at any time of the day.

These sweet kachoris are often called 'Gujjias' and are a 'must have' for the Holi festival. You can store these for several days in an air-tight container.

For the dough (crust)
1 cup plain flour (maida)
2 tablespoons melted ghee
a pinch of salt

To be mixed into a filling
½ cup (75 grams) khoya (mava), grated
5 to 6 almonds, sliced
5 to 6 pistachios, sliced
½ teaspoon cardamom (elaichi) powder
1 tablespoon sultanas (kismis)
1 tablespoon sugar
a few saffron strands

For the sugar syrup
1 cup (200 grams) sugar
½ cup water
a few saffron strands

Other ingredients
ghee or oil for deep frying

For the garnish
a few saffron strands
chopped pistachios

For the dough (crust)

1. Combine all the ingredients and knead into a firm dough using enough water. Knead well for approx. 5 to 7 minutes.
2. Allow the dough to rest under a damp muslin cloth for 10 to 15 minutes.
3. Divide the dough into 12 equal portions. Keep aside.

For the sugar syrup

1. Dissolve the sugar in ½ cup of water and boil the syrup for 4 to 5 minutes.
2. Add the saffron and mix well.

How to proceed

1. Divide the filling into 6 equal portions.
2. Roll out each portion of the dough into a 75 mm. (3") diameter circle.
3. Place a portion of the filling in the centre of one dough circle. Cover with another dough circle and seal the ends completely using a little water (refer to the first diagram below).
4. Turn the edges of the kachori (as shown in the first diagram).
5. Repeat for the remaining dough circles and filling to make 5 more kachoris.
6. Deep fry the kachoris in hot ghee over a slow flame till the kachoris turn golden brown in colour. These take a long time to fry as the crust is thick and needs to be cooked on the inside also.
7. Drain on absorbent paper and allow the kachoris to cool slightly.
8. Dip the kachoris in the hot syrup. Drain and keep aside.
   Serve garnished with saffron strands and pistachios.

handy tips
1. You can make 12 half moon shaped kachoris or gujjias using the same recipe (as shown in the second diagram on the next page).
2. You can even serve these kachoris without dipping them in sugar syrup.

Diagrams on next page

Diagram 1

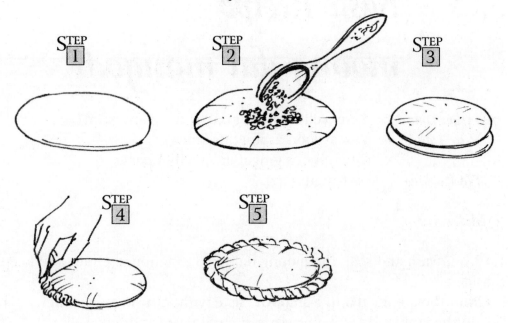

STEP 1   STEP 2   STEP 3

STEP 4   STEP 5

Diagram 2

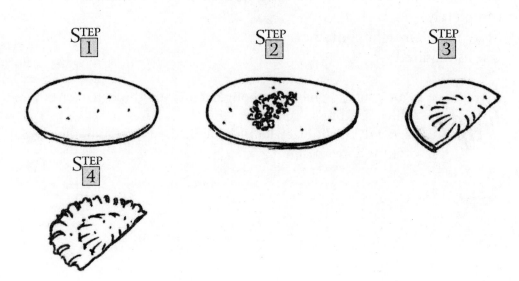

STEP 1   STEP 2   STEP 3

STEP 4

Basic Recipe
moong dal mangodi

Preparation time :
2 to 3 days.

No Cooking:

Makes 1 cup.

1 cup yellow moong dal (split yellow gram)
½ teaspoon asafoetida (hing)
2 teaspoons ginger-green chilli paste
oil for greasing

1. Clean, wash and soak the moong dal for 6 to 8 hours. Drain and keep aside.
2. Grind the moong dal to a smooth paste without using any water.
3. Add the asafoetida and ginger-green chilli paste and mix well.
4. Put the mixture in a piping bag fitted with a plain nozzle and pipe out small dots on a greased thali.
5. Keep the mangodis in the sun for 2 days or until the mangodis dry out completely.
6. Store in an air-tight container.
   Use as required.

handy tip

1. You can also pipe the moong dal mixture through a 'chakli' or a thick 'sev' press.
2. Urad dal (split black lentils) can be used instead of moong dal for the above recipe.